MW01065442

MEANINGFUL CONNECTIONS:
A PERSONAL RETROSPECTIVE

HARRY W. STONECIPHER

Steindorff Press

Carbondale, Illinois, March 1995

OTHER BOOKS BY THE AUTHOR

Editorial and Persuasive Writing

Electronic Age News Editing
  with Douglas A. Anderson
  and Edward C. Nicholls

The Mass Media and the Law in Illinois
  with Robert Trager

Published in the United States by Steindorff Press, a division of JEM Communications, Inc., March 1995.

ISBN 1-879776-08-1

Illustrations by Armen B. Sarrafian

This book is dedicated to my wife and partner of fifty-five years, Helen Marie Lenty Stonecipher. While her assistance in producing this manuscript was invaluable, she should not be held responsible for any of the views expressed herein.

If you would not be forgotten,
As soon as you are dead and rotten,
Either write things worth reading,
Or do things worth the writing.

—Benjamin Franklin
Poor Richard's Almanac
May 1738

Table of Contents

Introduction

T o begin at the beginning, the impetus for these scribblings came during a recent drive around Camelback Mountain in Phoenix with my favorite niece, Beverly, at the wheel of a leased Mercedes sedan. Somewhere between a tour of the Desert Botanical Garden, where the 100 degree-plus October heat reminded my wife and me that we were no longer in Southern Illinois, and a stop at the plush but elegant Phoenician Resort in Paradise Valley built by Charles Keating, the flamboyant financier now serving a prison term for fraud, my niece interrupted my rambling reminiscing about boyhood experiences in Southern Illinois.

"Why don't you write some of this stuff down?" she asked. "I would like for my children to be able to share one day how things were when you and my dad were growing up."

Ordinarily such a suggestion would have been soon forgotten, but this request caught me in a state of retrospection. My wife, Helen, and I had driven to Scottsdale to attend a reunion of my

World War II Army outfit, the 33rd Infantry Division, my first such "Golden Cross" reunion. Reflection about events reaching back more than fifty years with scores of combat veterans, most of them now seventy years of age or older, is enough to bring on a reflecting high. We had visited earlier in the week with two former university associates now teaching at Arizona State University in Tempe, which served to reinforce all those past academic connections. And we had swapped newspaper stories with a couple of former publishing friends now retired in Arizona.

Suddenly these connections—family, military, publishing, academic—all seemed more interconnected than ever before. Indeed, in retrospect, experiences that once seemed one of a kind and isolated, now appeared more interrelated. During the long four-day drive back to Illinois, my niece's suggestion stirred long dormant thoughts and memories of boyhood years, of growing up on tenant farms during the Great Depression, of sometimes joyous relationships with two younger brothers, of frequent troublesome relations with a hard working and driven father, and of a loving and caring mother we all took for granted. These and a flood of more recent connections and experiences that flowed from those beginnings tempted me to respond positively.

Indeed, it might even be fun, I reasoned, to try

to capture some insights of these experiences in a record others might be interested in reading. After all, I had been a journalist, and I do have some experience in putting words on paper. Then, too, it was my favorite niece who was asking for such an effort. So first, I will be writing for you, Beverly, perhaps with more detail than you ever wanted to know, but I hope that there may be others who also might be interested: family members, friends, professional associates, perhaps some I may not even know or remember. Anyway, after seventy-five years, it seems a privilege to be embarking on such a retrospective journey, wherever it may lead.

In case others stumble upon these pages, it occurs to me that perceptive readers may wonder just who this person is who merits—if that's the right word—being the focus of such an outpouring of personal retrospection. And if Beverly is indeed the niece of the writer, a proclaimed Southern Illinoisan, what's she doing way out there in the Arizona desert?

Well, my niece is by all accounts a bright, energetic, competitive young professional woman in her mid-forties who some might say "has it all." She is a physician, wife of an ophthalmologist, a mother of three, a housewife, family administrator and financial planner, and a political activist, the latter set off by President Bill Clinton's proposal for health care reform. She was the first of her family to go to college and has encouraged her younger brothers and sisters to further their education. She is a caring daughter of a father back in Illinois who has suffered for years with diabetes and more recently with Parkinson's disease and who, along with other siblings who can afford to do so, has contributed to meeting the costs of his mounting health care needs.

Beverly is currently frustrated with a host of family problems, including efforts to encourage her eldest son to finish college, even if it takes a fifth or sixth year, and in helping to elect a second Republican U.S. senator from Arizona who might be more oriented toward the concerns of health care providers in the ongoing battle to reform the system. She goes at all these activities and tasks, professional or otherwise, with gusto. How could an uncle and former reporter not be impressed by this niece who can stir up more things worthy of a news report in the span of a few days than can a half dozen ordinary citizens?

These little essays that follow are dedicated to Beverly, who may not agree with all the ideas and views expressed but who will, I trust, appreciate the effort put forth in producing them. It's already clear to me that it's going to be more difficult to write meaningfully about one's memories and personal experiences than to report on the activities of others as a news reporter. But such an effort seems worthy and doable. We shall see.

My last endeavor toward supporting a livelihood before retirement ten years ago was a fifteen-year stint as a journalism teacher at Southern Illinois University at Carbondale. Communication theory often crept into the lectures and readings for such courses as "Writing for the Mass Media" and "Critical and Persuasive Writing," which I taught regularly. I even managed to convince the university administration from time to time that I was enough of a scholar to warrant promotion with research and publication related to my teaching, including a textbook expounding the process of editorial and persuasive writing. But in my teaching, I soon learned that any social science research finding into the process and effects of mass communications is tentative at best.

One communications problem lies with the reporter, whether a student cub reporter or a professional who witnesses the event about which he or she writes, or who gathers information from others about such an event or happening. To put it into social science terms: "No one perceives everything that there is 'out there' to be perceived," a process called "selective perception." And such selectivity is said to be "functional," that is "the objects that play the major role in the organized perception, the objects that are accentuated, are usually those objects which serve some immediate purpose of the perceiving individual." All of which might help explain what one can recall and cannot recall years later about the perceived meaningful events in one's life.

My very earliest memory that I can tie any date to is the birth of my youngest brother, Haney, who is Beverly's father, which occurred when I was only four, if I can rely upon my birth certificate. Now, more than seventy years later, I clearly recall that I and my middle brother, Amos, were locked out of the farm house and told to play in the front yard during most of the day by those who were apparently attending my mother. I don't remember the doctor who was in attendance or anything about my father, who must have been around somewhere. For whatever reason, however, I distinctly remember being barred from the house and somehow sensing that this was no ordinary day. Strangely, I don't remember ever seeing my new baby brother that day or feeling threatened by his introduction as a new member of the family. This farm house still stands just west of the Bell Missionary Baptist Church where my parents and grandparents from both sides of the family are now buried. The open front porch of the house where a swing was once the center of activity has now been enclosed, but the grassy front yard still looks much the same as it must have looked on September 30, 1922, Haney's birth date.

I have only one other memory of the farmstead, which I'm told was also the birthplace of Amos and me as well, though my birth certificate lists the location of my birth as Haines Township, and that there was a little spring at the bottom of a knoll in a nearby pasture where cool water flowed throughout the hot summers. I have often wondered if that spring is still active or if, long since, it has dried up as the result of some more recent environmental problem. If a long life teaches anything, it is that everything is in some sort of process and is ever changing. I'm reminded that so many changes experienced by seniors can dry up long lasting relationships and connections, but that is a story reserved for later.

Though my earliest memory is the birth of your father, Beverly, I'm not at all sure what "function" such a retrospective perception serves, but I want to examine a number of meaningful personal connections in the pages that follow, some having to do directly with family, for example, the German connection of family members as descendants of Johannes Steinseiffer who was born in Eisenfeld, Germany, in 1692 or 1695 and came to America in 1749. Then there is the marital connection that for Helen and me now spans more than half a century; the military connection that somehow has tied the life of a young, seventeen-year-old farm lad who lied about his age to get a position paying $21 a month plus room and board to a seventy-five-year-old retired Army officer; the publishing connection involving community newspapers, which was at the center of both our careers for many years; the on-again, off-again academic connection that would today be called nontraditional at best; the religious connection, which might be characterized as leaning toward Christian agnosticism; and that developing senior citizen connection that tends to be a leveler with people sharing all kinds of common problems—and ailments—being generally accepted for what they are without reference to any previous rank, title, or occupational or professional role.

In examining such meaningful connections, of course, it may become more clear how the one is related to the other or what effect one may have had on the other. As one grows older, it becomes more apparent that all life experiences are interconnected. Even what one sees and doesn't see, for example, may depend on earlier experiences. Three eyewitnesses to an automobile accident will see different things depending upon their experience, which tends to bolster the old adage that an eyewitness isn't necessarily a reliable witness. This doesn't mean, however, that one of life's meaningful connections necessarily has a cause and effect relationship with another such connection.

In a lecture on verbal and statistical fallacies in

a course entitled "Critical and Persuasive Writing," I used to cite David Hume, the British philosopher, who maintained that for a cause and effect relationship to be established three conditions must be met: (1) The cause must precede or be simultaneous with the effect, (2) there must be some more or less clear connection in time and space between the two events being causally connected, and (3) there must be what Hume called a "history of regularity" in the first two conditions. Statistical correlation between lung cancer and cigarette smoking might be acceptable as an instance of causal reasoning because it does satisfy Hume's three conditions. The types of relationships to be examined in the pages that follow, however, probably fail to meet Hume's criteria. Experiences are personal and one of a kind; memories are difficult to quantify.

In reminiscing recently with former World War II Army buddies in Scottsdale, one perceptive veteran remarked that we all seemed to remember different things about our combat experiences and even suggested that, perhaps, our stories had grown in both length and heroics as the years have passed. He concluded that, while he didn't remember all the events in the stories being recounted, he himself tended to remember most of the "good stuff." I trust that the facts in the pages that follow are mostly the truth and that they have escaped such embellishment, but these facts are mixed with opinion and ideas that tend to be neither true nor false. Opinion and ideas may be viewed as either good or bad, but they are not generally subject to any test of truth. The reader may, of course, either accept them or reject them.

And even when one can be fairly sure that things remembered really happened, it's still difficult, looking back after five or six decades, to be sure just when they occurred. It certainly is easier to think in a straight line when one is actively engaged in an event than when one looks back retrospectively. Don't count on a chronological approach in the pages that follow. In reflecting on past events, there is yet another problem and that is what once seemed real, in retrospect, may now more easily be questioned. A journalist tends to grow more skeptical through the years, it is claimed by some in the profession, because he or she is lied to so frequently by politicians and others seeking a favorable press report. One doesn't need to be a reporter, however, to grow more skeptical in accepting the recommendations and opinions of others; indeed, it may be injurious to one's health not to develop a healthy skepticism about all types of messages and appeals whether they come from advertisers, politicians, preachers, even one's teachers.

In any event, it is hoped that the reflections and

views that follow, while limited by selective perception and perhaps tainted with skepticism by one who has already exceeded the insurance actuarial tables of life expectancy, will contain at least some of the "good stuff" that every full life should produce. But then, that concept itself may be subject to selective perception. We shall see.

The Family Connection

I was born just four days after the armistice was signed ending World War I, and my father, being an ardent Democrat, came up with a middle name for me to reflect his political bias and, as presidents go, Woodrow Wilson is a credit to most. An older sister, Ruby, still needed the family cradle, and according to my mother a beer crate became my nesting place. She related this to me years later when I was deeply involved in religious activities. I think she told this with a certain degree of pride in my new-found orientation, but I suspect that she was also reminding me of my lowly beginnings.

Little Ruby, as she was called, couldn't have used that cradle for long after I was born because she died in 1919 during an influenza epidemic that took thousands of lives that year across the United States. She was buried in an unmarked grave in the nearby cemetery of Bell Missionary Baptist Church. I have always wished that she had lived; I would have liked a sister. I have always imagined that growing up with a sister would have brought a better understanding of girls—and women. In death she has remained forever Little Ruby. For my parents, however, her memory became a frequent point of contention, sometimes even causing hostility between them, which I never fully understood until years later.

That contention was expressed, in part, in a continuing argument over the need to mark Little Ruby's grave with a proper headstone or monument. I remember my mother raising the subject time after time and, for reasons I didn't understand, the marker—though sometimes promised—was never purchased by my father. Each renewed request seemed to pick up where the last argument ended. As the years passed, I often wondered why my mother just didn't buy the marker on her own and have it placed on the grave. My father often placed the source of such family problems on mom's stubbornness.

Years later when my father was in a nursing home for a few days following hospitalization, my mother, then in her eighties, one day turned our conversation to girlhood memories, of growing up on a farm near the old Stonecipher place, of courtship with my father, of his beautiful horses—my father loved horses—of going to church together in a buggy, and suddenly, out of the blue, she said, "You know, we had to get married."

I don't remember how I responded, but I do

remember wanting to tell her, "Mom, it doesn't matter." But, of course, it did matter. It had apparently mattered to both her and my father all those years; that, in no small part, was what the arguments over a marker for Little Ruby's grave had been about. And I wanted to say, "No, Mom, I didn't know." But that was irrelevant because she knew or feared that family members and girlhood friends and acquaintances did, indeed, know, and that it was a matter of record, and a source of shame, and a cause for blame. Our conversation that day forced me to think of my parents for the first time in romantic terms and to realize how different courtships must have been back then. Suddenly learning what others may have known for decades about that courtship, however, did not damage or lessen the significance of family bonds for me. In fact, thinking of my parents as a couple of young people courting in a buggy and feeling romantic toward one another has done just the opposite—bound my family ties even more closely.

When my father died a couple of years later, my mother finally accomplished her mission. Helen and I accompanied her when she picked out a massive grey stone which, beautifully engraved, now marks both their graves in the Bell Baptist Church Cemetery. Alongside their monument is a small headstone, an acknowledgment of Little Ruby's existence and my mother's stubbornness, which simply reads, "Ruby Ellen Stonecipher, 1917-1919."

During the early years, moving must have been an accepted part of living for my parents; they certainly did a lot of it. Sometime before I was to enter grammar school, we moved from the farm in Haines Township to Salem, Illinois. I still remember glimpses of those first days at Central School in Salem and what then seemed to be a huge gymnasium on the upper floor of the building. My father had been employed in the shops of the C&EI (Chicago and Eastern Illinois) Railroad. I remember visiting the big roundhouse where the steam locomotives were serviced and could be swung around on a huge turntable. I would go with my father to watch baseball practice near the shops where dozens of players in their clean, colorful uniforms warmed up for the game. I don't remember my father playing on the team, but he must have practiced or had some function there.

I also remember being taunted at school with shouts of "Scab, Scab," words I did not understand until my mother explained that my father and hundreds of others had been employed to replace previous workers who had struck the railroad. Years later I was to become a member of two different labor unions, but I have never had to walk a picket line nor had my job threatened because of such actions. Had these occurred, I wonder if I too would have taunted others with such an expletive.

The financial debacle of 1929 ended my father's railroad job; it also brought about another move, this time back to the farm in Haines Township south of Salem where my father grew up. My grandmother, by then a widow, moved to Salem to live with a daughter, my aunt Grace, and her family, and my parents were suddenly farmers again by necessity rather than by choice. I was eleven, and despite the hard work that followed there was an excitement for a boy growing up on the farm in those days, but more about that later.

During the next six years, my parents moved three more times, and each move got more and more complicated and difficult. I remember the midwinter move from Haines Township to a farm four miles south of Salem when I was an eighth grader. The weather was cold and the move was made by wagon and on foot over fourteen miles of sometimes muddy, sometimes frozen, rutted roads. Moving the furniture and household belongings was the easy part of the venture; it was the long treks two or three times a week hauling ear corn, loose hay from field stacks, crates of chickens, farm machinery, and other trappings, and the frustration of herding livestock along country roads that was difficult. The move stretched over several weeks, but the promise of rich bottom land to farm and the convenience of living closer to a town such as Salem gave my parents new hope.

Within the next year or two, my parents bought and moved to a small farm just to the east of this tenant farm with the bottom land, the first real estate they had owned, I think, since their marriage. But even this last move brought few living comforts. There was no indoor plumbing and there was no electricity, though the REA (the Rural Electrification Administration) would soon bring service to area homes. The new home did have a cistern near enough to the back corner of the house that a hand pump had been installed in the kitchen and water could be pumped from within, providing the pump remained primed. This was the last house we lived in as a family. After graduating from high school, I joined the Army at the age of seventeen and, except for short intervals, never lived at home again.

Helen and I drove out to visit the old homestead recently. The unoccupied two-story frame building, located a mile off the mail route on a dirt road now dead-ended by Interstate 57, stands in disrepair. The front door was ajar, the building surrounded by overgrown evergreens, the driveway blocked by fallen limbs. The interstate, which split the farm diagonally when it was built during the 1960s, runs through what once was our pasture with its preponderance of blackberry bushes, which were once the source of delicious pies at the hands of my mother. An interstate rest stop has been carved into the only wooded area. Eighteen wheelers now idle on concrete ramps with their diesel exhausts fouling the air where I and my brothers enjoyed the shade on hot days.

When my parents bought the farm almost sixty years ago, not another house existed between the farm and our mailbox a mile to the east. A group of fox hunters from Salem often sat around a campfire alongside the road near the top of a knoll, usually on Saturday nights, and listened to the hounds bay as they chased the wily fox through neighboring fields. During the war years when my father was working at the shops in Mount Vernon, which were busy with war contracts, my mother would walk the long mile each day to get the mail from her sons in the military service. Half a dozen houses, most of them small, some in disrepair, now mark the road, but most of the residents were gone this day, perhaps to their work in Salem or Mount Vernon. After all these years, things were no longer the same, and I recalled the sadness in the words of Thomas Wolfe: You can't go home again.

Historians now call the early 1930s the years of the Great Depression but, as a boy of eleven or twelve, I don't remember feeling poor or under-privileged. Maybe it was because, as a Southern Illinois farm boy, most of those I knew in school and elsewhere were equally poor. It was years later that I came to appreciate the struggle my parents must have had during those years to provide for three growing sons. I do recall arguments about our attendance at school when often, as my father would argue, our efforts were needed in the fields or for chores around the farm, but my mother would usually prevail. Indeed, when it came time for me to begin high school, she insisted that each of us get a high school diploma. Looking back, I don't see how they managed financially, but the hardships we suffered now seem to be more a badge of honor than a matter of deprivation.

That first year on the old Stonecipher place, to which we moved when I was eleven, seemed to be particularly tough. I remember my father rigging a board seat on the walking cultivator tongue that summer with brother Amos, who had just turned nine, riding and driving the team of huge horses while I walked behind and manned the cultivator handles. The idea was to dislodge the weeds by navigating the shovels as close to the row as one dared without plowing up the row of corn. But Amos, of course, had the easier job. At the time, I always thought of Amos as my father's favorite. Part of the problem may have been that as the eldest son I was destined to catch many of the more difficult tasks, but that perspective came much later.

There were always weeds to hoe between the

corn rows, and hundreds of cockleburs and morning glory vines, which never seemed to stop
sprouting, particularly in the rich bottom land
During the off season, there was the task of cutting
and clearing brush and saplings from fields and
fence rows, especially sassafras, which seemed to
grow everywhere. During the late fall and winter,
there was the constant need to cut wood for heat-
ing with the crosscut saw, and to husk corn, often
in cold snowy weather during the Thanksgiving
and Christmas holidays from school.

Other boyhood tasks were, in hindsight at
least, more interesting and memorable. Butchering
day was such an event maybe because it always
involved a neighbor or two and was generally
marked by frantic activity. The hog had to be killed
in a certain manner, bled, scalded, cleaned, and
drawn in a set time frame to guarantee success.
Despite the excitement of the butchering process,
I could not eat directly afterward when there was
usually an immediate meal of brains or liver or of
some other organ that could not be preserved
readily. In the spring, the butchering process was
completed as the hams were smoked for days in a
little building aptly called the smokehouse.

I remember also what now seems a quaint
practice of burying vegetables such as turnips and
sweet potatoes to preserve them during the long
winter months. To store such vegetables above

ground in those days brought the danger of freezing, even if stored indoors. But the success of the bury depended upon making it deep enough for the vegetables to escape the winter freeze while providing sufficient drainage with a surrounding moat to avoid winter rains and snows. It was apparently an interesting challenge for my father; sometimes it worked, sometimes it didn't.

Most of the manual labor was in the fields, but there were at least two tasks around the house that I and my brothers tried to avoid, generally without success. One was being drafted to help my mother on wash day. Without electricity, the washing machine functioned by turning a hand crank. Fifty strokes—full turns of the handle—here, a hundred there as directed by my mother. Even then the washboard had to be used for very dirty clothes.

The garden was also in my mother's realm. My father usually plowed and prepared the ground of a large garden plot near the house, but from that point on it was my mother's project. Again, one of us boys was often drafted to assist in the planting and hoeing of lettuce, radishes, carrots, beans, cabbage, sweet potatoes, sometimes sweet corn and melons. This was primarily a garden to supply food for the table, but my mother usually found room for a few flowers: poppies, daisies, snapdragons, petunias, sweet peas, marigolds, zinnias, sometimes a row or two of bulbs producing crocuses, daffodils, tulips, irises, or lilies. But it was in the house, not the garden, that my mother more often demonstrated her green thumb with vines and pots of flowers everywhere.

In those early years I can remember a lot of talk about physical ailments. My father suffered from asthma for most of his adult life; my mother's ailments were generally linked to liver trouble—her diagnosis. I remember the concern of both my parents for brother Haney's lack of growth in those early years. He was often referred to as the runt, but a stint in the Marine Corps as an aerial gunner during World War II turned that problem around.

Brother Amos suffered for years with something then referred to as the croup, and I remember my mother sitting up with him long hours in the middle of the night. I'm not sure how the malady was overcome; perhaps he finally just outgrew it. The most serious childhood sickness I can remember was scarlet fever. I still shudder when I think of those large pills I would gag on. I still find it difficult to even swallow an aspirin unless it is coated. We survived those years even with no mention of health insurance or a regular family doctor.

The dominant memory of those early family years, however, was that as a teenager I really didn't like my father very much, and I assumed that the feeling was mutual. In my memory, he picked on me with extra work, which often seemed to be punishment. I thought he was critical of much that I did, often in language befitting a top sergeant—which I was later to become—criticism my brothers seemed to escape. And sometimes he did things that seemed so grossly unfair that I felt I couldn't tolerate it any longer.

As a freshman or sophomore in high school, for example, I had a project of a sow and litter to meet the requirements for one of my agriculture courses. Vocational agriculture was a common concentration of study in high school for farm boys in those days. The vocational agriculture teacher visited each student's farm during the school year, checking on the progress of each project. When I came home from school one day to find my sow missing and later learned that she had been shipped to the stockyards in East St. Louis for auction, I was crushed and angry. I'm not sure now what my father's explanation was, but it fell short of meeting my outrage.

A night or two later, I packed some food and a few articles in a towel, crept out of the house after everyone was asleep, and ran off! I walked the four miles to Salem, caught a westbound freight train headed for East St. Louis, began to get hungry the following day when my food ran out and was nearly killed catching another moving freight a short time later, this one eastbound toward home. But the train didn't stop in Salem, and I ended up in

Olney, from which I finally hitched a ride back to Salem after standing along the highway for what seemed an eternity.

After all these years, I still remember the hunger pangs of nearly three days without food, but at that time I couldn't bring myself to beg for a handout. The whistle of a freight train would years later remind me of being whipped violently around the end of that boxcar in East St. Louis and hearing the wheels grinding on the steel rails below me. I had not only misjudged the speed of the train, I had also caught the ladder at the wrong end of the boxcar—a near fatal mistake. I expected harsh treatment when I finally straggled back home on foot, but my mother treated me as a prodigal son. I don't remember a word from my father.

There were other manifestations of my lingering anger toward my father. Years later in college in a course in advanced fiction writing, I remember writing a short story about a boy who went hunting with his father's dog along a beautiful and secluded stretch of a wooded creek not unlike Crooked Creek that ran through my father's farm. At some point, as the dog poised on the opposite bank in anticipation of the hunt, the boy raised his gun and shot the dog. With an agonizing yelp, the dog fell into the swift water with blood rising to the surface as the poor dog's body first sank and then rose to be swept away by the current. There was a lot more, but that was the gist of the story, which the professor viewed as rather strange for a college student to be writing, even a nontraditional student such as I. It was more than strange, it was scary because I was that boy.

Years later, however, I learned to better appreciate my father's efforts during those depression years to provide for our family's welfare, and I recall walks we took together where I listened as he talked about people he had known, which he always assumed I would remember. He was approaching eighty then and these frequent walks alongside the city reservoir and around the nearby hospital were therapy for his wobbly legs, and the talks were good for his mental health—at least he seemed to be cheered up by them. But I enjoyed those walks and talks also. We never talked of anything particularly personal; he was not one to express regrets about things that may have gone wrong in the past. But, in retrospect, I think he did regret them.

Stonecipher

The German Connection

The family surname was first Steinseiffer or Steinseifer. It originated from the name of a small village in extreme East Germany, Steinseifersdorff, which dates back to 772 A.D., located in the Erzgebirge Mountains between what used to be Czechoslovakia and Germany. The villagers began to move into the Seigen District of Westfalen located in Old Saxon perhaps as early as 1250 A.D., according to a family history published in 1986 entitled *The Descendants of Johannes Steinseiffer*. At that early date, the villagers had no last names, but as the need for identification increased they adopted a surname from their ancestral village.

The name Steinseiffer also is occupational in origin. Indeed, the village of Steinseifersdorff was called the Stone Polishers Village. Another source indicates that as a result of onomastic research the surname means "one who polishes semiprecious stones." A present day coat of arms produced by Halbert's *Library of Arms* shows a shield in the traditional colors of gold with three blue cornflowers surrounded by eight semiprecious stones.

The first Steinseiffers settled in the small town
of Eiserfeld, which is mentioned as early as 1255
A.D. in old documents. There is a photograph in
The Descendants of the ancestral home of the
Steinseiffer clan built perhaps as early as 1255,
according to one report. The photo of the house
was submitted to the compiler of the family history by Emmey Steinseifer who, in 1971 at the age of
seventy-eight, described herself as "the last living
Steinseifer" in Eiserfeld. Emmey, a descendant of
Johannes, was the last occupant of the house located on Bergstrasse, the oldest street in Eiserfeld,
before it was torn down in 1964 to make room for
a parsonage. Johannes was born in this historic
house in 1692; so were his eight children. He and
his wife, Elizabeth, and seven of those children
departed from Eiserfeld in 1749 to come to America, but more of that history later.

When the Steinseiffers began migrating to
America in the mid-1700s, they were required, or
at least encouraged, by British law to Anglicize
their names. Some of the family, however, continued to cling to some aspects of the old German
forms. In Maryland and Pennsylvania, for example, the last part of the name became "sifer," copy-
ing from the German, while in Tennessee some
kept the first part of the German by spelling it
Steincipher. Stonecipher is the most Americanized

version of the name, but in England even today it is spelled as Stonecypher. Many clan members in North Carolina, Georgia, Alabama, and Mississippi, likewise, use the surname Stonecypher.

The religion of these early clan immigrants was German Reformed, according to *The Descendants*, at least the ones who came to America. Since they lived in the Erzgebirge Mountain area, however, they were probably influenced by the preaching of John Huss, which was Baptist in principle, but were called Husites by their religious enemies. From 1720 to 1750, Governor Spotsworth of colonial Virginia recruited many Germans to come to America to work in the iron mines. It was work in the mines in Culpeper County, Virginia, that probably attracted Johannes Steinseiffer in 1749, who was to become the German connection to the American branch of the family. It was Johannes who became the starting point for the 254-page history of the American clan compiled in *The Descendants*. By my calculations, Johannes, that first generation ancestor, was my great-great-great-great-great-grandfather. For short, let's call him Gramps I.

Unfortunately the three principal editors of the family history soon found so many descendants of Gramps I that their research was cut short and the findings were published in 1986 by a fourth editor and compiler, Harry Sheldon Stonecipher of

Helenwood, Tennessee, ending with the sixth generation of my branch of the family—that of my
grandfather. It's these six grandfathers who interested me most in this long, sometimes confusing
and uneven genealogy attempting to trace the
descendants of Johannes Steinseiffer in America.

It's difficult to understand what would prompt
a German family of some means almost 250 years
ago to pull up stakes and set sail for a new home in
colonial America halfway around the globe. It certainly took courage, perhaps a sense of adventure,
and it took some means in 1749 for a fifty-four-
year-old father to book passage on a sailing ship
called Patience for his wife and seven children.

Four years later, their eighth and oldest son,
Johann Heinrich (John Henry), my Gramps II,
took the ship Edinburg to America. The ship
record showed his age to be twenty-eight. *The
Descendants* speculates that Johann may have been
in the German Army at the time the rest of his family immigrated. Both ships discharged their passengers in Philadelphia from where the Steinseiffers proceeded to Culpeper, Virginia. The records
indicate that Johannes purchased 200 acres of land
in Culpeper County. He died just eight years later
at the age of sixty-four and was buried in the German Reformed Church cemetery there.

One thing that can be said about the early
Steinseiffers is that they were prolific. Johann

Heinrich, Gramps II, the oldest of eight children, was married three times and was the father of seven children, five girls and two sons, all born in Culpeper County. The tax and census reports, Revolutionary War records, and his will were less than clear about vital statistics, but the family moved to Wilkes County, North Carolina, about 1773. No time of death is recorded, but his will was probated in 1816, indicating that he perhaps reached the ripe old age of ninety.

Joseph Steinseiffer, the eldest son of Johann, my Gramps III, entered the Revolutionary War from Wilkes County, North Carolina, where he had moved with his parents around 1773. He served for three months as a volunteer, was discharged, later was drafted and, according to *The Descendants*, took part in several battles and skirmishes, one of the most notable being the Battle of Kings Mountain. His brother, John Henry, Jr., also served in the Revolutionary War. After the war, Joseph married Salome Rose in Wilkes County and fathered eight children, five sons and three daughters.

It was after the Revolutionary War that the family name was altered, first perhaps to Stinecipher and sometime later, one source suggests even after the Civil War, the name became Stonecipher. Sometime between 1803 and 1812, Joseph's family, along with his uncles and other relatives, moved to Morgan County, Tennessee. *The Descendants* reveals that there they purchased large holdings of land along the Emory and Little Emory rivers and two tributaries—Beach Fork and Crooked Fork creeks. Joseph died in 1847 at the age of ninety-three and was buried in Beech Fork Cemetery in an unmarked grave.

I can relate more closely to Ezra Stinecipher, the eldest son of Joseph and Salome, and my Gramps IV. Ezra was born on Lewis Fork in Wilkes County, North Carolina, January 1, 1782, but moved with his parents and seven brothers and sisters to Morgan County, Tennessee, in the early 1800s. There he met and married Susan Curtis, the daughter of Joshua Curtis, a Revolutionary War veteran. In 1814 or 1815, Ezra, a gunsmith by trade but a carpenter, furniture maker and farmer as well, built a three-story house of squared timbers in a beautiful valley seven miles south of Wartburg, Tennessee, just off present day Tennessee Route 62.

Helen and I first visited Ezra's home a few years ago while I was teaching at the University of Tennessee at Knoxville. We returned more recently for a photo session. Gramps certainly had an eye for beauty. The view down the valley from the front yard of the old house, until recently occupied by descendants of the family, is still striking even after 180 years. In 1814, before the intrusion of civilization, it must have been even more beautiful. Ezra died in 1838 near Hopkinsville, Kentucky, where he was buried. He and one of his sons had been to Southern Illinois, probably Haines Township, visiting relatives and to look at land to purchase. Ezra died on the way home to Tennessee.

My grandfathers to this point, it is interesting to note, had all been the first born in their families and, in the lexicon of most genealogists, their designation followed the same pattern 1.1, 2.1, 3.1, 4.1, setting out the generation in the first number, followed by the order of birth in the second. Samuel Stinecipher, Gramps V, the genesis of the Illinois branch of the family, however, was the fourth child of Ezra and Susan and was, therefore, labeled a 5.4.

The Descendants is saturated with Samuels through the years, but Samuel 5.4 was born January 24, 1814, in Morgan County, Tennessee. In 1835 he married Susan Ann Henderson; four years later the couple moved to Haines Township, Marion County, Illinois, where he bought 120 acres of land from the federal government, later purchasing an additional 160 acres. The farm home he established was to become the home place for three generations of Stoneciphers. Pleasant Grove Missionary Baptist Church still stands on the southeast corner of the farm off Illinois Route 161 some fifteen miles east of Centralia on an acre of land Gramps gave for religious use.

Samuel, following the various crafts and trades of his father, was a gunsmith, blacksmith, furniture and buggy maker, as well as a farmer. Following the family tradition, he was a Baptist and a Democrat. Samuel and Susan had three sons before her death in 1848. Samuel later married Malinda Ross and they had five children, four sons and a daughter, the first born being my grandfather, Alexander. Samuel died on October 26, 1898, and was buried in Wham Hill Cemetery just a few miles west of Bell Baptist Church where later generations of Stoneciphers would be buried. The Wham Hill Cemetery, surrounded in part by a wrought iron fence, sets atop a knoll a quarter mile off the Cartter Road. Samuel's impressive monument carrying the name of a third wife, Mary Chance, whom he married late in life, stands near the rear of the cemetery, which is now filled with monuments carrying prominent family names familiar to generations of Southern Illinoisans.

Alexander Stonecipher, Gramps VI, died in 1926 when I was only eight years old, but I can remember visiting the old Stonecipher place when he was still alive. He and my grandmother, the former Mary Ellen Hill, had been married in 1878, and since my father was the youngest of six children they were quite elderly as grandparents go. After my grandfather died, I remember that a large, ornately framed photograph of him was displayed on an easel in the corner of grandmother's living room. I have a better memory of that framed picture than I do of grandfather. I remember also the row of trees that shaded the driveway to the house in the summertime and my grandmother insisting on kissing me and my brothers each time we visited, a wet kiss on the mouth, which I often tried to avoid without success. My grandparents are buried in Bell Baptist Church cemetery in a lot adjacent to that of my parents and Little Ruby.

The third generation of the family to live on the old Stonecipher home place, of course, was my parents who moved there after my father lost his job following the financial debacle in 1929, but that was for only a short time. For years now the farm has been in other hands, which somehow seems rather sad. The family heritage handed down from one's ancestors involves more than culture and tradition; it also involves the concept of place. That concept, I fear, is diminishing, indeed, may already be lost for many Americans today.

After publication of *The Descendants* in 1986, I became interested in updating the history of my grandfather's branch of the family. That on-again, off-again effort has produced a number of rewarding developments. Though my efforts have been more that of a reporter than a genealogist, I have had contacts with a number of researchers, including Arless Stonecipher of Georgetown, Tennessee, who has a computerized data bank that encompasses the extended Steinseiffer clan reaching back to his and my ninth great-grandfather in Germany. We share Johannes as Gramps I, but his Gramps II was Henericus, a brother of Johann Heinrich, my Gramps II. Arless is placing all the Stonecipher family information he can gather into this data bank, which will eventually be turned over to the Church of Latter Day Saints in Salt Lake City. Apparently, the Mormons have the largest such collection of genealogical materials in the United States. Arless' computer indicates that he and I are sixth cousins.

In 1987, Helen and I also enjoyed a visit in East Tennessee with Harry Sheldon Stonecipher, compiler of *The Descendants,* which had just been published. We poked around some of the ancestral haunts near Wartburg: a cemetery dominated by Stonecipher headstones and monuments and the historic home of Ezra, Gramps IV, a great-grandfather we share. Harry Sheldon has a son, Harry Curtis, a former CEO of Sundstrand, a $1.4 billion-a-year aerospace and industrial manufacturer in Rockford, Illinois, who was recently named CEO of McDonnell Douglas in St. Louis. Harry C. must be among the top moneymakers of the Stonecipher clan. Newspaper clippings indicate that his philanthropy has greatly benefited his

hometown of Oneida in East Tennessee. Arless'
computer indicates that Harry Curtis and I are
third cousins, twice removed.

Our visit to Wartburg that day had seemed like
a step back in time as we left Interstate 75 near
Knoxville and drove northwest along Tennessee
Route 62. Natural beauty soon surrounded us, and
the traffic thinned as the terrain became more hilly.
For several miles, we drove along a picturesque valley surrounded by tree-lined ridges dotted with
the sparse white blooms of dogwood. Wartburg
itself, a county seat town claiming fewer than a
thousand residents, resembled a movie set out of
the past that might have been at rest on the back
lot of Warner Brothers. This, then, had been the
base of operation for the Stonecipher clan who had
migrated to Illinois a century and a half ago. It
seemed that little had changed through the years.

In contrast, fifty miles to the southeast in Oak
Ridge, Tennessee, a thriving city of 30,000, visitors were being guided through eleven sites and
attractions to showcase the city's history, scientific
orientation, and commitment to the arts. Cloaked
in secrecy during the war years, Oak Ridge was the
site of the Manhattan Project, the code name for
the atom bomb project that would end World War
II. At one site, visitors viewed a graphite reactor,
the world's oldest continuously operated nuclear
reactor, now a national historic landmark. Ironical-

ly, the technology that resulted from the Manhattan Project, though it may have ended one war, was to threaten the security of the western world for decades during the cold war with Russia and is now the focus of possible conflict on the Korean peninsula. Such is the heritage of East Tennessee for the Stoneciphers and the world.

Through the years, others have published and marketed books purporting to extend the Stonecipher family history. I recently purchased such a publication, *The World Book of Stoneciphers*, which does have a couple of interesting sections including the great migrations of man and how family surnames originated, but the publishers, Halbert's Family Heritage, appear more interested in selling coats of arms than in genealogy. The registry section of the book lists 616 Stoneciphers with mailing addresses out of a total estimated population of 2,036 from throughout the United States. One has the suspicion that the 616 were those who had listed telephone numbers. There is a good rendering of the Stonecipher coat of arms, however, which is reproduced at the opening of this chapter.

As a boy, I remember my father being asked about the origin of the family name occasionally, and he would give some vague response about his Irish or English ancestors, and perhaps there was some generational basis along the way for his answer, but I don't recall any reference by him to the family's German connection. I'm sure that he knew of the German spelling of the name because I recall seeing "Steinseiffer" in the family Bible my grandmother Stonecipher kept on her sewing table years ago. But like so many of his generation, the role of Germany as the enemy during World War I didn't encourage the acknowledgment of such ancestors.

The publication of *The Descendants* in 1986, however, opened up a connection to the past of which I had little knowledge before. More recently, Arless' computer has reached back into family records in Germany to the year 1599. That's digging deeply into history. But I'm reminded that, as an eighth generation of that first American immigrant, Johannes, in 1749, that the German bloodline is getting rather thin—the fraction is something like one over one hundred twenty-eight. And after seeing the movie *Schindler's List* about the holocaust recently, my father might have had the right approach in dealing with family history.

But back to updating grandfather's branch of the family. The work thus far indicates that my father and his five brothers and sisters, true to the Stonecipher heritage, have been both enterprising and prolific. Aunt Grace Brubaker, my father's older sister, for example, was the mother of seven children. Were she alive today, she could count nineteen grandchildren, twenty-two great-grandchildren, eighteen great-great-grandchildren, and two great-great-great-grandchildren. In the process of searching, I discovered and have visited with a first cousin who I didn't even know existed. For my father's branch of the family tree, however, it's brother Haney who has extended the clan with six children, fourteen grandchildren, and three great-grandchildren, representing generations nine through eleven in the scheme of the Steinseiffer family genealogy.

To that favorite niece, Beverly, if you are still with me, this, in a nutshell, is an abbreviated version of my and your family history. Looking backward, as a member of the ninth generation you must add one great to the five which I use in addressing Johannes Steinseiffer, Gramps I. Looking forward, you must acknowledge that, for those making up your branch of the family tree in the eleventh generation, you are now a grand aunt—and at the age of only forty-four.

The Marital Connection

Only recently did I get around to reading Dr. M. Scott Peck's best seller, *The Road Less Traveled*, which was published in 1978 and had garnered millions of readers before I discovered its secrets, particularly those regarding personal relationships. Dr. Peck, a practicing psychiatrist, finds the notion of "romantic love" to be a myth that traps young people into marriage. The experience of "falling in love," he suggests, has as one of its characteristics an illusion that the experience will last forever. The myth of romantic love tells us, Peck writes, that for every young man in the world there is a young woman who was "meant for him" and vice versa. And when we meet that person for whom we are intended, recognition comes through the fact that we "fall in love."

The myth holds, Dr. Peck suggests, that through such a match each of the lovers will be able to satisfy all of each other's needs and will, therefore, "live happily forever in perfect union and harmony." This is a misconception, Peck concludes, because falling in love is not an act of will.

Indeed, we are just as likely to fall in love with someone with whom we are obviously ill-matched as with someone more suitable. And any attempt to examine love, Peck argues, is to toy with mystery, attempting "to examine the unexaminable and to know the unknowable."

Dr. Peck had lots of other things to say about the myth of romantic love, all of which got me to thinking about that marital connection, which began for Helen and me more than a half century ago and which somehow has become the central focus of both our lives through the years, encompassing virtually all our activities.

That mystery of romantic love I first experienced in the spring of 1940 while working as a bread and pastry sales and delivery boy for Kohrig's Bakery in Salem, Illinois. I was hardly a boy; indeed, I was twenty-one and had spent a year in the U.S. Army Air Corps, which I didn't like and, as a result, had purchased a discharge after serving the minimum time at Scott Field near Belleville and later on DEML (Detached Enlisted Men's List) in Chicago. I had worked for almost two years at the bakery, living with the Kohrig family for much of that time in their residence above the bakery. But I suffered from what Dr. Peck would probably call "extreme shyness"; I didn't like to call on new customers and, during the height of the oil boom that was going on in the

Salem-Centralia area at that time, new businesses were opening almost every week. I must have been more a delivery boy than the sales person the Kohrigs would have wished.

I was particularly shy where young women were concerned; indeed, I have remained shy, sometimes painfully shy, all these seventy-five years. I later learned how better to mask this shyness. It's not efficacious to be viewed as a shy first sergeant, nor is shyness effective in gathering news as a reporter or in communicating with a classroom full of college journalism students I was later to face. But even in retirement, shyness often haunts me still.

I must have seemed particularly shy that spring day when I was approached by a pretty, petite brunette from the old *Salem Republican* newspaper on her rounds gathering news with pencil and notepad in hand. As I recall, I was busily removing bread from the rear of the panel truck for delivery to a restaurant along Main Street when she approached with a simple query, "Do you know any news today?"

I really didn't know at that time what she was after, but I let her explain that she was gathering information about visitations between residents who lived in the city and those who lived elsewhere as "personal items," and news about any other social events of public interest. I listened, balancing a tray of bread and buns on one shoulder. I must have been intrigued with her approach and my interest was piqued by her involvement with gathering the news because I overcame my shyness enough to suggest, with an uncharacteristic flirtatiousness that, though I didn't know any news then, I might come by for a visit with her some Saturday evening. It must not have taken long for me to muster up the courage to find her parents' home on South Lincoln Street because our first date was early in May, the weekend of the Kentucky Derby, a date which has become a sort of milepost—as Charles Kuralt, formerly of CBS, might label it—of our long relationship or as a metaphor of our race together through the years.

In retrospect, those next few months of court-ship were among the happiest periods of my life, a relationship largely relegated to the weekends because of the early wake-up call for me during the week, often as early as 3 a.m., in order for me to begin making deliveries to cafes and other shops, some of which opened around 5 o'clock. There was nothing very newsworthy about our activities despite my announced news mission: a movie now and then—admission at the Lyric was then 28 cents—a joy ride around town in my 1936 Ford coupe my only worldly possession of note later evaluated at $200, even a visit to Forest Park in St. Louis one weekend.

Despite the joy of courtship, shyness still limited our activities. We had no experience with eating
out, for example, and were both uncomfortable
when we attempted such forays. We joined other
couples a time or two on weekend trips, but our
circle of friends was small, which didn't seem
unusual at that time. What does appear clear, however, was that the activities of our courtship forced
each of us to battle our anxiety and gave us the
courage to deal with our shyness which, in psy-
chological terms, at least, threatened to limit our
lives. These fears and anxieties still linger to some
degree even today, but I like to think that we have
matured rather gracefully despite our shyness.

Something else happened that summer that
proved to be far more significant than either of us
had reason to suspect. After discharge from the
regular Army in 1937, I had been recruited and
had joined the Salem unit of the Illinois National
Guard, a rifle company. It was not a matter of patri-
otism or a wish to see the world, appeals often set
out in military recruitment posters; it was simply a
means of supplementing a rather meager paycheck
from the bakery. Company I had some seventy
enlisted men and three or four officers who drilled
one night a week for a day's pay and during the
summer went on active duty for two weeks.

That summer's active duty at Camp McCoy,
Wisconsin, was extended to three weeks, a harbin-

ger of things to come. But I don't recall any concern at the time that this extension of active duty might be linked to the war erupting on the European continent; indeed, Europe seemed far away to a Southern Illinois youth in 1940 who had just made corporal. Our attention was focused on more personal concerns. I remember that the hit song that summer was "Blueberry Hill," which became intertwined somehow with our romance. I heard a few bars of it recently in a commercial hyping the release of an oldies record, and the magic is still there. It was that summer also that "You Are My Sunshine" somehow became our song for one another, and it has remained so.

When my enlistment was up following the Wisconsin encampment, I signed up for another four-year hitch. Helen reminds me that this was done without any discussion with her; it just didn't seem that important at the time. During the summer, there had been talk about military preparedness, or more accurately the lack of preparedness, especially the unpreparedness of the National Guard. Ultimately six divisions of the Guard were designated as units to receive one year of active duty training, and the 33rd Infantry Division, of which Salem's Company I was a part, was one of those six divisions.

Suddenly this budding romance, which had been pursued rather leisurely during the summer, became more serious and intense. The first mobilization date was set for December 31. Our first decision was to delay any plans for marriage until my return, and Helen would pursue her work at the newspaper. As the date approached, however, the wedding date was moved up. We were married on Sunday, December 15, 1940, in the Trinity Methodist Church parsonage, Helen's church, attended the morning services following the brief ceremony, enjoyed Sunday dinner in the country prepared by my mother for the happy couple and the bride's parents, moved my belongings into our new quarters with Helen's parents later that day, and returned to our jobs on Monday morning.

As it turned out, Company I wasn't mobilized until March 5, 1941, and after that the unit was billeted in the local armory for some two weeks before being taken by train to Camp Forrest, Tennessee. These ten or eleven weeks together may not have achieved the "perfect union and harmony" Scott Peck discussed in *The Road Less Traveled*, but I don't recall any serious problem except for the anxiety over the pending separation. Had we known then that this military interlude would last almost five years rather than the scheduled twelve months, that anxiety would have been even greater.

Even though the circumstances of those early months—which grew into years—were unusual, or

perhaps because they were unusual, so many of the
patterns of behavior and the context of our relationship with each other have served as guides for
our lives together through the years. One of the
earliest such acts was the choice of appellations for
one another, which began in the exchange of letters during the three-week encampment in Wisconsin that summer of 1940. I'm not sure why I
chose "Sweetpea," but Helen had pointed out the
tender, sweet-blooming flower in her mother's garden during the summer, and that seemed an appropriate appellation for her. Helen chose "Sugar,"
but I have no idea how that name fits me.

For the next five years, letters addressed to
Sweetpea and Sugar crisscrossed the United States
and eventually the Pacific Ocean as the government attempted to do what it could to keep up the
morale of its troops. The names suited us fine but,
during the years that all mail written by troops
serving in combat areas was read and censored—
the Army said they were "examined"—by an officer of the enlisted man's unit, this first sergeant's (I
had been promoted) twice-weekly letters to his
Sweetpea must have seemed incongruent to his
military image as the top honcho of a rifle company. The occasion for such mail slowed after the
war, of course, but those appellations still grace
birthday and anniversary cards, and expressions of
love on Valentine's Day. Helen noted recently,

somewhat regretfully I thought, that she hadn't
been called Sweetpea very often lately. But she still
has those hundreds of war time letters from me
tucked away in an old Army footlocker.

Early in our marriage, Helen began keeping a
personal ledger, which later developed into a more
elaborate columnar journal, itemizing our income
and expenditures through the years. She has maintained these records, including the checkbook and
other financial records. Her accounting skills have
assisted us in many personal and business ventures
through the years and on one or two occasions
even helped keep the Internal Revenue Service at
bay. That first ledger, begun January 1, 1941, two
weeks after our marriage, indicates that our combined cash balance was $678.63. My salary from
the bakery—I had moved to Taylor's Bakery in
June of 1940—was $20 a week. Helen was earning
$10 a week at the newspaper. Our combined week-
ly take-home pay that January was $27.81.

Before Company 1 was mobilized, we traded
my 1936 Ford coupe to the local Chrysler dealer
for a $200 IOU, which was to be applied on a new
Plymouth after my one year of military service. It
was to be a bonanza for the dealer who made use of
that IOU for five years when the attack on Pearl
Harbor by the Japanese brought the United States
into World War II. And after that long wait, the
new 1945 Plymouth I eventually purchased turned

out to be a real lemon, but that's another story.

While our income seemed sparse in 1941, our expenses were also slim during those early years. Helen's ledger indicates that we spent a total of $35.86 during the month of January 1941 and $20 of that went to Helen's parents to apply toward grocery bills. One of us made an office visit to Dr. Logan, which cost $1; my haircuts were 35 cents; my weekly life insurance premium was 60 cents on a $1,000 policy and Helen's was 26 cents on $500. The ledger indicates that movies were perhaps the primary source of entertainment during those months. We went to the movie theater four times that January, three of those visits to see double features, at 56 cents a showing for both of us. On March 4, the evening before Company I was mobilized at the local armory, we saw the just released *Gone With the Wind*, which cost a walloping 55 cents for each of us and which played to a crowded theater.

Other experiences and patterns of behavior during those early years, upon retrospection, were later to open opportunities for both of us. After the war and an attempt at a union job in a steel fabrication plant, I joined Helen at the newspaper as an apprentice printer, taking a cut in pay for the opportunity to learn the printing trade. At my encouragement, Helen had taken me to visit the newspaper plant on one of our first dates. We still have a Linotype slug containing the words "Harry Loves Helen" that the operator, who was working overtime, got and handed me hot from the machine knowing that I would drop it. I later sat at that same machine learning its intricate keyboard as a part of my training. After finishing my apprenticeship, I became a journeyman printer, but I soon discovered that it was the creative end of publishing that I was most interested in—the writing, not the production.

After some four years, we both quit our jobs at the newspaper and Helen supported my academic efforts at the University of Missouri School of Journalism at Columbia as we joined thousands of married students who crowded campuses after the war. Her salary at various jobs supported us financially, supplementing the G.I. Bill provisions, and her proofreading and typing skills helped in so many other ways. It was said that such wives were working on their PHT (Putting Hubby Through) degree. This was during the Korean War and, while I wasn't called to active duty as were many other Reservists and National Guard members including brother Amos, I continued in various Reserve units, completing twenty years of service needed for retirement.

After I had received two degrees from the University of Missouri, we became newspaper publishers, first in Washington, Missouri, and later in

Arcola, Illinois, where we attempted to put our knowledge and skills to use as entrepreneurs. Helen's name was on the editorial masthead as co-publisher, and readers often read of her in the editor's column where she was referred to simply as "the brunette who runs the office." But after ten years in Arcola without a vacation, we sold the newspaper and took a month-long vacation in Alaska and a ten-day trip to Hawaii before I began study toward a doctorate while teaching journalism at Southern Illinois University-Carbondale. But more about our joint venture into these military, publishing, and academic connections in the chapters that follow.

There is a more personal aspect of any marital connection that one could argue shouldn't be dismissed and that is the sexual aspect. Begging a defense of shyness and a lack of material to write about, this discussion will be brief. First, our courtship involved no premarital sex, but honesty in reporting compels me to acknowledge that this was due more to Helen's high moral principles than to any moral certitude on my part. I can report also with some assurance that there has been no extramarital sex through the years and, therefore, nothing to report here. As to the sexual intimacy between two lovers who entered into matrimony more than fifty years ago, that is private and will remain so, which rules out any chance of this story becoming a bestseller.

A related question is frequently asked: "Do you have any children?" We have answered negatively to that question countless times through the years. Another more complex question is sometimes implied: "Why not?" The truth is that we set a pattern early in our marriage when a common-sense approach to family planning seemed to suggest that we wait until after my military service to seriously consider starting a family. When that anticipated year of separation stretched into five, with thirty months of that time separated by thousands of miles, such a decision was further delayed. After the war, and for various reasons, our careers simply took precedence over the establishment of a family.

We have often been asked if we miss not having children, and our response has sometimes varied. In truth, I suppose, one doesn't greatly miss what one has never had. And what about grandchildren? I remember, Beverly, that my father seemed to enjoy his granddaughters immensely, and that you were one of the objects of joy. But he didn't pay that much attention to his grandsons, perhaps because he had reared three sons. Which reminds me of a bumper sticker I saw recently which read, "If I had known that grandchildren were so much fun, I would have had them first."

The most meaningful social event of our long

marriage, without doubt, was our Golden Wedding Anniversary celebration on December 15, 1990. On most anniversaries through the years, we had managed a dinner together at a favorite restaurant with perhaps a glass of wine, the latter an uncommon thing for us. But Helen had warned earlier in the year that this fiftieth anniversary called for something more. I suggested a trip somewhere, perhaps a Caribbean cruise, but that would deny us the opportunity to share the occasion with family and friends. In the end, we put aside our reservations about cost and our long-felt reticence about self promotion and undue publicity and planned a reception at the SIUC Student Center on campus with a dinner to follow in the Old Main Room for some one hundred invited guests.

We knew that the middle of December wasn't the best time to be planning such an event. We had taken note, for example, that on our forty-ninth anniversary, which we had celebrated with an overnight trip to Evansville, Indiana, it had snowed and the temperature had dropped to eighteen degrees below zero. In addition, this was the time of year when most people were busy, particularly college students and faculty who were involved in final exams ending the fall semester. A number of our invitations were going to former journalism faculty colleagues and graduate students, many of whom were now teaching on other campuses.

We decided, however, to take the risk, telling ourselves that if nobody showed up for the affair we could always dine alone as usual. As it turned out, the weather cooperated, and though some invited faculty colleagues couldn't come because of the winding down of studies, and others would decline because of the rush of holiday activities, some ninety did show up and the celebration turned out to be an enjoyable reunion with family members, former workplace colleagues, and long-time friends.

Helen had worked for weeks on the planning. There were reservations to be made early in the year for the Student Center facilities and with Marriott, who had the food concession at the Center, for the reception, buffet dinner, and the anniversary cake. There had been no wedding cake fifty years ago, and now was the time for catching up. It was a three-tiered lemon chiffon cake, beautifully decorated with columns and, at Helen's request, two white doves fluttering atop. And Vince Huffman, a music teacher at Christopher High School, was engaged to entertain at the keyboard. There were invitations to be ordered, addressed, and placed in the mail. There was the publicity for newspapers in Arcola, Salem, and Carbondale.

As the responses were coming in, there were arrangements for out-of-town guests to stay overnight and decorations for the reception area and the Old Main Room. When the anniversary cards began arriving in the mail, a sense of anticipation was inevitable—and stress. The reception was set for 6 o'clock on Saturday with dinner to follow at 7. On Friday I spent most of the day in bed with a severe headache and pain in my neck and was too dizzy to stand. I became concerned about being able to even attend the planned festivities. Helen took me to the Carbondale Clinic that afternoon and I remember telling the doctor my predicament and that Helen might even kill me if I wasn't able to act as emcee and introduce the guests that next evening. Indeed, Helen and I would be the only persons present who even knew all the invited guests.

The doctor gave me a scare with his initial concern that I might be suffering from meningitis (two students at the University of Illinois had recently been diagnosed as having it), but after ruling that out he gave me a shot of Toradol and suggested that I return the following day at about the same time for another Toradol shot, which he said should keep me on my feet for at least six hours, long enough to last out the celebration. That was my condition approaching the biggest social event of our lives, and it wasn't very reassuring. Ironically, the day following the celebration, the headache and dizziness disappeared as if by magic.

What turned out to be most rewarding about

our fiftieth observance were the scores of cards and
other responses from longtime friends and former
associates and the sharing of memories. A former
employee wrote, "You were able to make all of us
feel connected, and it was interesting to know
when each person present was a part of your lives."
And it was that feeling of interconnectedness that
Helen and I also enjoyed as guests from the various
periods of our lives responded when they were
introduced following the dinner in the Old Main
Room.

My favorite niece, Beverly, who had flown in
from Scottsdale, Arizona, speaking for family
members present, set the tone of the many
responses to follow in sharing memories of her visits to Arcola as a school girl and "working" at the
newspaper.

George Kohrig of Salem, who I shared a room
with in his parents' living quarters above the bakery where I worked before the war, suggested to
those in attendance that we had "discovered girls"
together. We actually had double dated the girls
who were to become our wives.

Best friend Herman Branson of Salem told of
the good times he and Maxine had shared with us
for some forty-five years and noted that, while we
had moved around from town to town in Missouri
and Illinois during these years, they had moved
only once—across town. I remembered with grati-

tude that Maxine had helped keep things together in the Stonecipher household on two occasions while Helen was recovering from surgery.

The Bransons' daughter, Marcia Arnold, now a music teacher in the Hamilton, Ohio, schools, read a long narrative poem she had composed detailing our lives together, which ended as follows:

> And now the time has passed
> To end this poem at last
> May the next fifty years be even better
> But don't expect a rhyme next time
> You'll just get a letter!

Amy and Scott, Marcia and Ernie's children, brought along their textbooks to study for finals on Monday at Anderson University. Helen and I have since been on hand to see both graduate from Anderson. Amy is now studying at Fuller Theological Seminary in California and Scott has plans to study mortuary science in Cincinnati. As it has turned out, being best friends of the grandparents, Herman and Maxine, has brought the satisfaction of sharing in the accomplishments of their grandchildren as well.

The newspaper connection also proved to be a prominent part of our anniversary observance. On the memory table at the reception, where the accomplishments of one's children might be expected on such an occasion, newspaper files and other memorabilia from publishing days were displayed and two former employees spoke movingly of those publishing connections.

Mildred Dennis of Perry, Ohio, then an English teacher in Arcola High School and a columnist and feature writer for the *Record-Herald*, wanted everyone to know that her experience on the newspaper had impacted her life "greatly," and that she had gone on to write a similar personal column for the *Painesville* (Ohio) *Telegraph* for twenty-five years and to become the author of three books of personal essays. She presented a laminated Labor Day column from the *Telegraph* containing a paragraph about her former editor's persistent editing habits with a handwritten note at the bottom: "Harry—You'll never know how much you've influenced my writing. Even today, when I apply your measuring stick, it means one more revision. Thanks." And Vicky Rothrock Blaase, who worked in the front office as proofreader and teletypesetter, had high praise for her learning experience at the newspaper, especially for Helen's efforts as mentor and counselor.

Helen also received praise from Andy Kmetz of Champaign, the state personnel officer for USDA Soil Conservation Service and a retired Air Force colonel, who characterized her area clerk position for Area 7 in Carbondale as being much like that of a first sergeant in the military, functioning as a key link in the organization between workers in the field and the administrative staff in the state office, sealed his remarks with a kiss, which made Helen's day.

Professor George Brown, former director of the SIUC School of Journalism and noted for his one liners, shared a few tongue-in-cheek thoughts on the art of teaching and some of the less serious aspects of higher education, probably for the benefit of faculty members in attendance, ending up somehow talking about the importance of teamwork. He surmised that Harry and Helen were a team that "somehow worked."

And though the hour was getting late for out-of-town guests, the most unusual responses probably came from the last two speakers. Kyu Ho Youm, a South Korean graduate student at SIUC whom I had supervised during both his master's and doctoral work, told of his ten years in the United States and had high praise for Harry and Helen who he called his "American parents." He proudly introduced his wife, Bokim, and their two sons, both namesakes: Harry Dershowitz Youm, then seven, and Eugene Stonecipher Youm, then three. The two had already popped up at many of the tables that evening and seemed to be enjoying the party. The Youms, who had flown in from Coral Gables, Florida, where he then taught at the University of Miami, were among visitors the following morning for brunch at 305 Canterbury Drive.

Dr. Robert J. Hastings of Springfield, Illinois, a Baptist minister who Helen worked with while the *Illinois Baptist*, which he edited, was published in Carbondale, topped off the evening's activities. Two of Hastings' many books, *Tinyburg Tales* and *Tinyburg Revisited*, were filled with humorous happenings in and around the mythical village of Tinyburg which, according to Hastings, "is located just a little bit south of Pretense." His presentation that evening was a new fictional Tinyburg tale from his word processor dealing with the *Arcola Record-Herald* and its two former co-publishers, Harry and Helen, and two historical figures who happened to be journalists. They were John Gruelle born in Arcola, who created the Raggedy Ann doll while working as a cartoonist at the *Indianapolis* (Ind.) *Star*, and James Whitcomb Riley, who had worked for the *Indianapolis Journal* but was better known outside Indiana as a poet.

It was a delightful story, too involved to be reported here, but we enjoyed listening once again to an audio tape recording of the evening's program recently. Dr. Hastings is an excellent practitioner of the storytelling art. Fifty years is a long time to recap in one evening, but after returning home that evening with all the balloons and flowers and other leftovers from the party, it seemed to us that things hadn't gone too badly.

In retrospect, I think that Scott Peck may be correct, however, when he states that any attempt to examine the concept of love is to toy with mystery. I fear that this feeble attempt to examine our marital connection, which has endured for more than fifty years and is interconnected with virtually everything that we have done or continue to do, may suffer from the same problem. And there may be myths surrounding the concept of romantic love, as Peck suggests, but the process of falling in love is no myth.

The passion of youth may have waned through the years, but the mystery and romance of tackling problems together, of setting and working toward realistic and challenging goals, of striving to win the various games we humans play, and in assisting others who through misfortune can no longer even enter the race, all these efforts and others can be so much more enriching and enduring with the companionship that is part of that marital connection.

Dr. Peck may be correct also when he states that falling in love is not an act of will and that we are just as likely to fall in love with someone with whom we are obviously ill matched as with someone more suitable. I can only conclude that I am indeed lucky to have made such a wise choice in a marital partner, for which I am most grateful.

Ironically, one of my former graduate students in a letter expressing his regrets at being unable to attend our fiftieth anniversary observance, noted that his ongoing divorce proceeding and a disrupting change in his lifestyle prevented him from returning to Illinois. His letter closed, "Please accept my sincere apology for not making the journey and my heartfelt congratulations at the beauty the both of you show the world whenever a person wonders if the institution of marriage is a viable concept. Whenever I wonder if a couple can actually make a marriage work, all I do is to think of the two of you. Your marriage represents the ideal that individuals like me can point to and say, yes indeed, it can work." Thanks, Mike, for the kind words.

I'm encouraged that, though Scott Peck warns that life can be difficult and that life may be complex, with such recognition adversity can be overcome, which should give hope for all of us.

The Military Connection

It took a war to get most of the young men of my generation involved in the military, and at war's end most of them gladly departed the armed forces. But that was not true in my case, and looking back on those early years I think two things coalesced at the time I graduated from high school in June of 1936 that drew me into military service. One was the element of adventure, to which I think many youth respond; in my case it was an attraction to flying, which was relatively new in those days for a Midwest farm boy. A number of pulp magazines in the 1930s carried stories about aerial dog fights of flying aces during World War I. I remember particularly stories about the exploits of the French escadrille, which excited my imagination about flying. The only airplane I had even flown in was a lumbering two-engine Ford that took on passengers in the open fields near the Porter Lumber Yard at the south edge of Salem.

The other condition that made the military attractive was the depressed economy, which made employment virtually nonexistent for a boy of seventeen. I had worked intermittently that summer at a neighbor's farm while he was involved with the WPA (Workers Progress Administration). The pay was a dollar a day. I also signed up in the local National Guard unit, Company I, whose members received a day's military pay for one evening's drill each week at the local armory. When the farm job disappeared in the fall, I hitchhiked to St. Louis and enlisted in the U.S. Army Air Corps for four years with an assignment to Scott Field near Belleville, Illinois.

An Army private in 1936 drew $21 a month, plus room and board. But even obtaining such a position didn't come easily; in the first place, I was only seventeen, and second, I have a hammer toe. My parents, at my urging, signed that I was eighteen and, after a recruiter in Marion, Illinois, had turned me down because of the toe, I hitched a ride to St. Louis, went to the downtown Federal Building where I underwent a physical, and rode a streetcar up and down Broadway half a dozen times back and forth from Jefferson Barracks awaiting my acceptance, which finally came on October 29, just two weeks before my eighteenth birthday. Finally, I had a job and there were airplanes around, a lot of airplanes. There were also a number of lighter-than-air craft, the airmen called them "blimps," which I hadn't counted on and which I would see a lot more of than I would the airplanes.

That was the beginning of a military connection that was to last some twenty years, a total of seven on active duty and the rest as a member of the National Guard and later in the U.S. Army Reserves. Military experience brought growth and opportunity in a way I would never have imagined: a growing appreciation of discipline and team work, the development of skills and broad work experience, and educational opportunities in both the military and later in civilian pursuits. The military also brought loneliness and separation from family and unexpected temptations and risks, including the killing fields encountered by all combat infantrymen. Had I read *All Quiet on the Western Front* as a seventeen year old I might not have been so elated by the adventures of the French escadrille during World War I. But death and dying aren't foremost in the thinking of a teenager, which is probably a good thing.

My primary assignment at Scott Field was personnel clerk, but I remember long hours on guard duty in the middle of the night and being called out time after time at all hours to help pull in the huge lighter-than-air craft or to help launch one on a training flight. There was some opportunity for schooling: parachute rigging, airplane mechanics, and perhaps others. I lost interest in parachute rigging when I learned that the final exam was to rig your chute and jump with it. I passed the aptitude exam for air mechanics school only to learn that there was then no quota to attend the six-month course at Chanute Field near Rantoul, Illinois.

When the newness of military activities wore off, barracks living became quite lonesome and, although Salem was only fifty miles away, passes were infrequent and transportation for me was by hitchhiking. I learned that I could purchase a discharge at the end of one year, but I knew $125 wasn't going to be easy to save. I learned also that it was the officers who flew the airplanes, but I did manage to catch rides from time to time on training flights. Near the end of that year, I was transferred to Sixth Corps Headquarters in Chicago where I worked as a clerk in what was then called the Old Post Office Building and where I developed a lasting dislike for large cities. I was happy to be discharged November 10, 1937, as a private first class.

Upon returning home the following year, I worked at various farm jobs before landing a job at Kohrig's Bakery in Salem. In the meantime, I was back in the National Guard, this time as a corporal. When the 33rd Infantry Division was federalized March 5, 1941, for a year of training, I found myself on active duty once again. This time there was no opportunity to purchase a discharge. Quite to the contrary, when the Japanese attacked Pearl Harbor on December 7, 1941, our term of service was automatically extended "for the duration."

During the first weeks of the mobilization, I had been made the first sergeant of Company I, primarily, I think, because the company commander thought I was smart enough to keep the morning report and duty roster and to maintain the huge set of Army Regulations. But I soon learned that a lot more than administrative duties was needed to hang on to those first sergeant stripes, and for some of those line duties I was ill prepared.

In retrospect, one of the interesting aspects of those five years of active duty during World War II was to act as an unofficial liaison between the 103 enlisted men inducted from the Salem area with Company I and their relatives and friends back home through both news reports and, sometimes, personal correspondence. I ran across the draft of a news story in my footlocker recently that I had written for the *Salem Republican*, where Helen worked, which was published as a front page story relating the various military encounters and the efforts of Company I members. The dateline was Kobe, Honshu, Japan, September 25, 1945. It was written in longhand and filled twelve pages.

The story told of being moved out of Camp Forrest, Tennessee, after the declaration of war, first to guard the power installations around Knoxville, Tennessee, and later the shipyards near Mobile, Alabama. During the next several months,

Company I was stationed at Fort Sill, Oklahoma, Fort Lewis, Washington, and Camp Clipper, a tent camp in the desert of Southern California. Many of the original members of the company had left the organization. Nineteen had successfully qualified for commissions in the Army—brother Amos was one of these—two for the Navy, and one as warrant officer. Others had left on cadres to form new combat units. Indeed, there were only thirteen members of the original company left when the 33rd Division sailed for overseas from Camp Stoneman, California, on June 20, 1943.

My story related the movement of Company I during the next thirty months: Hawaii, for guard duty and jungle training; Finschhafen, New Guinea, where the division saw combat for the first time; Morotai, Netherlands East Indies, to hold off Japanese attacks against the island's only airport; Lingayen Gulf, Luzon, the Philippines, where months of intensive combat followed as Company I moved fifty miles through mountainous terrain to the north toward Baguio, the summer capital of Luzon; and finally on to Japan, after that country surrendered, as part of the occupation troops.

The news story, which had been cleared after some editing by division public information officers, went on to relate pertinent details about the various engagements in which Company I took part. I was an officer and a combat veteran by that time, but as a news reporter I was a beginner. For a cub, it wasn't a bad report. Reading the story now, I am surprised that I've forgotten so many of the things reported, but other aspects of those skirmishes will never be forgotten.

My most vivid memory focuses on a bloody two-day battle for Question Mark Hill, one of the first assaults in the Philippines in which Company I was involved. The company had scrambled up Question Mark that February morning in only a few hours, but it was the hanging on that presented problems. Cut off from the rest of the battalion, fighting without water or food for two days, and suffering heavy casualties, it was a rude introduction to mountain combat. Eleven officers and enlisted men were killed, twenty were wounded, and countless others suffered from heat exhaustion and battle fatigue. Late on the second day, reinforcements finally arrived and Company I was ordered to withdraw.

That night on Question Mark was the longest and most frightening of my life. The company dug in upon reaching high ground but, by the time darkness fell, the Japanese had closed in around us. I shared a foxhole with Alan J. Kennedy, the company commander, a redheaded, slightly built Irish captain from Portland, Oregon, and one of the bravest officers I have ever encountered. He was all over the company perimeter that night and never received a scratch. I can still see him sitting on the edge of our foxhole in the semidarkness pleading on the field telephone for our artillery to be brought in closer to our lines in an effort to keep the Japanese from overrunning us.

Kennedy later studied for the priesthood in Colorado and was returned to his beloved Portland where he still serves in retirement. I also remember the dead, particularly the body of my favorite platoon sergeant, Charles L. Whitlock, one of the original members of Company I, who was killed just a few feet from our foxhole. His body lay there for the duration of our fight and was buried along with the others in a mass grave, later to be exhumed by a grave registration unit.

A fourth printing of *The Golden Cross: A History of the 33rd Infantry Division in World War II*, compiled by the 33rd Infantry Division Historical Committee, was published in March 1994. A copy, which includes activities of the 130th Regiment and the battle for Question Mark Hill, has been placed in the Carbondale Public Library.

Following such engagements, enlisted men in the battalion were not allowed to write about the fighting, but newspapers back home were filled with reports of the continuing assault on Baguio, which Helen dutifully clipped and pasted in her scrapbook. The headlines during the next several weeks in Illinois newspapers boasted about the Illinois division's efforts. "Illinois Fighting Yanks Win Glory on Luzon," "33rd Division in Gun Range of Japs at Baguio," and "Retreating Japs Lose Supplies to Illinois Troops." The *Salem Republican*, in a special dispatch from the Philippines, carried a front page story under a four-column head: "Question Mark Hill Won by Salem's Company I." A few days later there was a small story headed "Company I Top Kick at Question Mark Hill Commissioned Second Lieutenant."

A field commission, or "battlefield commission" as it was popularly called, was just that. The commanding general of the division, in a surprise visit to the area, pinned on the gold bars of a second lieutenant in the field. His stated belief was that a noncommissioned officer with combat experience was more apt to survive future combat than a "new shavetail" fresh from the States. Shortly after that I was assigned to the First Battalion as an intelligence officer, "responsible to the battalion commander for the collection, evaluation, and dissemination of all enemy information and material." I was later to learn that it also included leading patrols to probe enemy lines. I had resisted officer candidate school for almost four years and still had misgivings about becoming an officer. And as I was to learn later, I had also unknowingly extended my overseas duty by giving up my enlisted status.

The First Battalion saw plenty of combat during the next few months and suffered many casualties. My intelligence platoon, made up of both enlisted men and Filipino guerrillas, was hit particularly hard in April when one of our incendiary mortar rounds fell short and burst above our positions. I can still smell the burning flesh and hear the cries of pain as those hit attempted to stop the burning by pouring the limited water in their canteens on their wounds. A few days later we were to engage in a task force to push the enemy from his dug-in position north of Baguio. I remember the stench of the bodies of dead Japanese strewn along the trail as we advanced. As a part of the intelligence mission, we searched the bodies of enemy dead for evidence of unit designation or of their military mission. Photos from some of those bodies made their way into my photo albums, snapshots of Japanese family groups, other more formal poses of Japanese soldiers in military uniform, some perhaps of those whose bodies we had searched. I have often wished these photos could be returned to the Japanese families involved, but that would be virtually impossible to do.

It's ironic that the bloodiest battle for me as an officer would also bring the highest accolade. It was a couple of months after the task force battle that I was presented with a Silver Star for gallantry

by the commanding general of the 33rd Division
in front of a regimental formation. General Order
117, dated 11 June 1945, read in part: "Acting as
assistant commander of a task force, whose leading
elements had received intense enemy machine gun
and rifle fire, Lieutenant Stonecipher was called
upon to lead two platoons of guerrillas in an
attempt to outflank the enemy strong point. Notic-
ing the reluctance of the guerrillas to leave their
positions of cover under the severe enemy fire,
Lieutenant Stonecipher, at the risk of his life,
exposed himself to enemy fire and by this act of
courage inspired the guerrillas to follow him. He
led them gallantly in the flanking attack, killing 15
enemy riflemen and knocking out the two enemy
machine guns which were holding up the advance
of the task force. By his gallantry under severe enemy fire and his fine display of leadership, Lieutenant Stonecipher contributed in a large measure
to the annihilation of the enemy strong point."

The task force commander engaged in a bit of
puffery in writing this citation, of course, but the
embellishments made my role sound "gallant"
when read in later news reports. At the time, however, I was more concerned with the never ceasing
tide of war. Indeed, just a month following this
engagement, I was the lone casualty in a skirmish
of my intelligence platoon with a Japanese patrol
north of Baguio. Somehow I had escaped being hit

in a number of previous engagements when we were all at greater risk. Why was I being singled out now?

In retrospect, I suppose that I was beginning to feel that it wasn't going to happen to me, and when it did, it shook me up. The apparent randomness of who is hit and who escapes—once that thought takes hold, it becomes frightening. I can still remember the fear that gripped me that night in the field hospital lying flat on my back with a twelve-inch wound up my left thigh listening to the artillery shells going over and not knowing if the hospital might be overrun in some unexpected counterattack. I felt helpless, the night was dark, my leg throbbed from pain, and I felt all alone.

The war was never quite the same after that. My letter to Helen the next day from my hospital bed gave a more upbeat report. After noting I had undergone two hours of surgery to repair the leg wound, I promised to save the 9-millimeter bullet, dug from my posterior, as a souvenir. The account contained nary a word about my fear, but it does contain several details long forgotten:

"I was out on a patrol and me and my Filipino guerrilla came out on a ridge kind of by ourselves and we spotted a Jap patrol right down the wood-ed draw from us. We could see them and they had-n't seen us as yet so we didn't want to holler at the rest of the patrol. I put a grenade on them and killed one and all hell broke loose. We both shot one more and a third one was killed by the Filipino. By the way, all I had was my pistol. We held off the rest of the Japs until our patrol arrived. I was dueling with a Jap officer—he had a pistol also. He was a rotten shot though. He must have fired twenty times and only hit me once. We had the advantage over them for we were on top of the hill and they were below us. You can tell that from the way the bullet started at the knee and came up. Just a minute—time out for a shot."

When I returned to the writing, probably realizing that such an account wasn't going to be very comforting to Helen, I suggested that I was going to be out of action for several weeks—it turned out to be forty days. I signed off acknowledging that it was Decoration Day and that the Kentucky Derby, the fifth anniversary of our first date, had recently been run again. According to my Officer's Qualification Card, as the result of being wounded in action I was awarded the Purple Heart while still a patient in the 92nd Evacuation Hospital near Baguio recovering from my wounds. Helen has always thought the colorful medal was "pretty"; for the past several years a representation of the Purple Heart has decorated our special issue Illinois auto license plates.

After release from the hospital, I received the additional duty of Plans and Training Officer with the responsibility of planning activities and training for all battalion personnel not engaged in the line. The job involved doing as well as planning, which brought about another perilous encounter, this time with fragments of one of our own rifle grenades. I was supervising a field firing exercise of an assault team armed with bazookas, flame throwers, and a squad armed with M-l rifles equipped with grenades when a grenade, fired by an enlisted team member, fell short and exploded. Several fragments tore into my jacket with one embedding itself deep in my left elbow. Only one enlisted man was injured.

Back to the hospital once again, this time for twenty days, I had plenty of opportunity to ponder my bad luck—or was it that my luck had run out. In retrospect, I remember the joy of hearing reports on August 6 from my hospital bed of an atomic bomb being dropped on Hiroshima, Japan, the first such bomb to be used in warfare, and a few days later a similar bombing of Nagasaki, another Japanese city. Little did we know that the powerful forces unleashed in those two attacks would haunt world powers for decades to come. All it meant to us at the time was that perhaps the war would soon be over and, with my bad run of luck, it wasn't coming any too soon.

My letters to Helen during the next several weeks were filled with optimism that the war might

soon be over. On August 28, I wrote an upbeat letter about being welcomed back from the hospital
by officers of the battalion and receiving the Silver
Star from the commanding general following a regimental parade. But all was not well: The Japanese
had delayed their arrival in Manila to surrender
formally to General Douglas MacArthur and,
although enlisted men with eighty-eight points
were being returned to the States for discharge,
officers with eighty-eight or more points, including me, were to be retained.

Indeed, the First Battalion shipped out of
Luzon on September 20, 1945, and landed in
Wakayoma, Honshu, Japan, three days later. The
battalion ended up in Himeji where I was to spend
the next six weeks engaged in taking over various
military facilities in preparation for the occupation.
I recall the difficulty in working through inter-
preters and with all the bowing and curtsies, which
soon became annoying. My letters to Helen were
filled with anti-Japanese expressions, which seem
unwarranted, even embarrassing to read today. But
feelings of animosity toward things Japanese linger.
I set out to buy a Honda Accord several years ago,
but I couldn't bring myself to do it, which had
nothing to do with the quality of the automobile.

It was on Armistice Day that I finally arrived
back in the States with a contingent of 33rd Division officers. After a few days at Vancouver Bar-

racks in Washington state, we traveled by train to St. Louis where we were met by Brigadier General Robert W. Davis, then publisher of the *Carbondale Free Press*, who had been regimental commander when the 33rd Division was inducted in March of 1941. It was just a few days before Thanksgiving and, though we were detained at Jefferson Barracks awaiting discharge, it was a joyous homecoming. The next day I took a streetcar up Broadway to meet Helen at the bus station; after a thirty-month separation, it was an emotional reunion.

The Army held on to us for several days more, but with Helen at a downtown hotel the military discipline and regimen soon faded. Indeed, I declared that I was ready to quit the military forever. But a few days later as I signed the separation papers, which called for a twenty-one-day leave, I was encouraged to sign up for Reserve status. Why not? There was no requirement for military drills or other such obligations. This proved to be true for two or three years, but as the threat of Communism increased during the cold war the effort of the military to remain prepared also increased. But more of this later.

Those first few weeks at home were busy and exciting. First, there was the matter of getting a job. Brother Amos, who had arrived home at about the same time after fighting the war in Europe with the armored field artillery and who had raced across

the continent with General George Patton's
armored divisions, accompanied me on a couple of
job interviews. I found a job with a steel fabrication company making oil field storage tanks, a job
I soon came to dislike. Amos took a job with a
Caterpillar sales and service plant where his military training had uniquely prepared him for a successful career. He later was called up for military
service during the Korean War and finally retired
from the National Guard as a brigadier general.

And a note to my favorite niece, Beverly, if you
are still following this tale. Brother Haney, who was
discharged from Company I before we were mobilized back in 1941, ended up joining the U.S.
Marine Corps and fought the war in the Pacific as
an aerial gunner. We corresponded from time to
time, but we never got together during those long
months even though we both served near one
another in the Southwest Pacific. This had nothing to do with the fact that the Army and Marines
didn't get along well, which indeed they didn't.

At one period in 1943, I remember that members of the 130th Infantry Regiment and the
Marines were restricted to different Hawaiian
towns when they went on pass. Another point of
contention was that the Marines seemed to get
most of the publicity and the credit when it came
to fighting the Pacific War. Marine outfits would
often sail forth from Hawaii, engage the enemy in

some remote Pacific island, and within a few days or weeks arrive back in Hawaii for furloughs to the States before the next engagement. Indeed, my mother became convinced that it was the Marines and your father, Beverly, who were winning the war in the Pacific and she wondered what I was doing over there for so long.

I remained in the Reserves in an unassigned status until mid-1949, when concern for military preparedness brought pressure on such Reservists to join a unit or resign our commissions. I followed the lead of other area Reserve officers and joined a detachment in Centralia. After beginning study at the University of Missouri in Columbia in the fall of 1950, I joined the 420th Military Government Company in nearby Jefferson City, Missouri. Many Reservists were called to fight in the Korean War, but the 420th was never called.

I finished out my twenty years in the military in the 5037th Army Reserve School in Champaign, Illinois, while Helen and I published the *Arcola Record-Herald*, a community newspaper we purchased in 1957, retiring as a captain in 1960. During these years I went on active duty for two weeks each summer at such installations as Fort Leonard Wood, Missouri; Camp McCoy, Wisconsin; Fort Benjamin Harrison, Indiana; with the last tour of active duty, ironically, at Fort Benning, Georgia, location of the Infantry School, which I as an infantry officer was seeing for the first time.

My retirement, however, had more to do with pressing newspaper duties than on any dissatisfaction with the military. I was forty-one in the summer of 1960, and it would be a long time—some nineteen years—before I was eligible to begin receiving retirement pay, but that wasn't the reason I had remained in the military.

Military service had made possible many other pursuits for me—schooling, publishing, teaching— and has been interrelated with so many other interests. But despite long association with the military, I'm uncomfortable with today's superpatriots. I'm distrustful also of those who are too quick to advocate solving international problems through military action. Military combat is about fighting and killing and dying, and though there may be issues worth dying for, they are surely limited. The real problem, of course, is that it is the young who must do the fighting and dying. If wars in the future had to be fought by politicians and generals, there likely would be fewer of them. Despite such views, as I wake up each morning to KMOX radio in St. Louis and listen to the martial music, often a march that highlights the hour, I still get a twinge of excitement and, despite my arthritic knees, my feet seem ready to step out again on one of those parade reviews so characteristic of the military.

But more touching still, and perhaps more thematic of the military, are the lonesome notes of a bugler playing "Taps." I stood with some two hundred others recently in a memorial service for departed comrades of the 33rd Infantry Division in the closing session of a reunion held at the Safari Resort in Scottsdale, Arizona. In one segment of the service, following the soulful singing of "My Buddy," those attending were asked to call out the names of recently deceased members. Many names were called, sometimes in unison, and a bell would ring three times. This went on for some eight or ten minutes. Then the bugle sounded "Taps." I didn't know most of those named by comrades, but tears welled up in my eyes, not for those recent dead whose names had been called, but rather for all those 33rd Division soldiers who had died in combat some fifty years ago in New Guinea, Morotai, and the Philippines before their lives had hardly begun.

The Publishing Connection

I learned the printing trade as an apprentice at the old *Salem Republican*, an Illinois semi-weekly, in the years following World War II and, like printers since colonial times, I too dreamed of someday owning my own newspaper. Benjamin Franklin had done it back in the eighteenth century after serving an apprenticeship with his brother, James, on the *New England Courant*. Indeed, most colonial publishers were printers by trade before becoming publishers. But I also knew that one needed to know far more than the backshop to survive as a twentieth century publisher.

Many community publishers in the 1940s had learned their skills working as reporters and editors for the daily press. Weimar Jones, a former city newspaperman, acted on his dream of owning a weekly newspaper in 1945 when he and his wife moved back to North Carolina where they purchased the *Franklin Press*. He later wrote a little book, *My Affair With a Weekly*, about his experience, which still has a prominent place on my bookshelf.

I also knew about the careers of two intriguing community editors who took quite a different approach—let's call it the academic route. One was Henry Beetle Hough, publisher of the *Vineyard Gazette* on Martha's Vineyard. Hough and his wife, Elizabeth, purchased the paper in 1920 shortly after they both had graduated from Columbia University's Graduate School of Journalism endowed by Joseph Pulitzer. Hough edited the *Gazette* for sixty-five years before his death in 1985 at the age of eighty-eight. His book, *Country Editor*, which I treasure, has become one of the most widely read books about community newspapering. Helen and I enjoyed a visit to the *Gazette* shop and to Martha's Vineyard several years ago. The paper is now owned by James Reston, a syndicated political columnist and former associate editor of the *New York Times*.

It was publication of the autobiography of William Allen White in 1946, however, that really whetted my appetite for journalism and newspapering. White had begun as an apprentice printer, had worked at various newspaper jobs while in college, including writing for the *Kansas City Star*, before purchasing the *Emporia Gazette* in Emporia, Kansas, in 1885. The *Gazette* was to become one of the most famous small-town newspapers in America and its editor a powerful voice in national politics before his death in 1944. White was a keen observer of small-town life with a flair for narrative and a lively sense of humor. I've often thought that every small town should have such a newspaper editor. That conviction was reinforced when Helen and I visited Emporia during my college days. Unfortunately, the world of journalism has produced few Henry Beetle Houghs and William Allen Whites, but their newspaper careers have been an inspiration to me.

Even as an apprentice printer in Salem, I had become a correspondent for the *Decatur Herald* and a stringer for the United Press wire service. At the *Herald*, I was paid by the column inch, and I had to paste up the stories as they were published. I don't remember how much I was paid, but I remember getting a monthly check once for more than $30, which included a story I had done about William Jennings Bryan, who was born in Salem. I called in my news to the United Press bureau in Herrin and was paid whatever they wanted to pay, which wasn't much. But the experience gave me a taste of journalism, and I liked it.

Looking back, it isn't surprising that as soon as my four-year printing apprenticeship was completed, Helen and I quit our jobs at the *Salem Republican*, placed an ad to rent our new home on South Lincoln Street, and moved to Columbia, Missouri, where I entered the School of Journalism at the University of Missouri in the fall of 1950. At the same time I began part-time work as a journeyman printer at the downtown paper, the *Columbia Tribune*, and Helen sought employment to support my academic efforts. The move surprised family and friends, some of whom questioned our sanity.

It was work at the university paper, the *Missourian*, however, that gave me and many other World War II veterans then attending school under the G.I. Bill the opportunity to learn the skills needed to become newspaper reporters and editors. The paper served as a laboratory for students, but it was also a daily newspaper of general circulation that competed with the downtown *Tribune* where I worked as a printer each afternoon and on Saturday mornings.

As a student in a reporting class, I remember spending two hours each morning making the rounds at the Boone County Courthouse, which was within walking distance of the campus, and writing the news I gathered for publication that afternoon. Likewise, editorials written by students in the persuasive writing class were submitted to the *Missourian* for publication if considered worthy by the faculty editor. There was no student editor at the *Missourian*. The paper at that time was located in the basement of the classroom building, and the huge letterpress would shake the building when it started its press run each afternoon.

Of even more interest to me was a series of

courses taught by a faculty member who was also the manager of the Missouri Press Association, which had offices in an adjoining journalism building. Upon completing the courses, students were required to participate in a field exercise to produce the weekly edition of an area newspaper. I still remember those days spent in St. Joseph, Missouri, with a retired Army colonel and a young woman from South America, which must have seemed a strange team of student journalists to townspeople. We first sold advertising for the upcoming edition, then gathered the news, wrote and edited the stories, and supervised the production of the paper. The publisher left town and turned it over to us. It was a heady experience as we sought to please both our instructor and the courageous publisher.

As school was winding down, Helen and I began our search for a weekly newspaper to purchase in the classified section of the *Publishers' Auxiliary*, at that time the trade paper printers and journalists alike turned to for employment and newspaper listings. We were corresponding with editors and visiting select newspapers in Illinois, Kentucky, and Missouri as I was finishing my thesis and continuing work as a printer at the *Tribune*. Some papers on the market were found to be too expensive; some of the towns were unattractive; some of the properties had been misrepresented in the advertising. After I received a master's degree in January of 1955, I began full-time work at the *Tribune*, but our newspaper search intensified.

Five months later we closed a sale and moved to Washington, Missouri, noted nationally for its production of corncob pipes, and took over publication of the *Citizen*, one of the newspapers I had surveyed in my master's thesis entitled, "Editorials and Personal Columns in Missouri Weeklies." For the next thirteen months, we were to become involved in a whirlwind of activities and an accelerated learning experience that would change the course of both our careers.

Washington, a town of 7,500, was perched on the south bank of the Missouri River some fifty miles southwest of St. Louis. We were attracted to the culture of the city, which flowed from its German and French ancestry; we were fascinated—at least initially—by the river; we had immediately liked the seventy-four-year-old publisher who had been a co-founder of the *Citizen* in 1905 and had been its sole owner and editor since 1937; and we learned that we could afford the paper and could see ourselves as publishers in Washington. What we didn't count on was the strength of the competing *Missourian*, but more on that later. We took over the reins of the *Citizen* on July 1; I was thirty-six years old and the *Citizen* was approaching fifty.

The following week, in a front page statement, the retiring publisher, George Krumsick, said his goodbyes to readers and welcomed the new owners. The new editor bragged a little about the community and its business leaders and concluded, "These first few weeks will be trying and perhaps not without mistakes in spite of the best efforts and guidance of Mr. Krumsick. Your cooperation will be needed and appreciated. The result of our combined efforts will not only improve your newspaper, the *Citizen*, but will boost, we believe, the best interests of Washington as well."

Part of that improvement meant upgrading the production process. Within a week or two, a second Linotype was purchased. The lead paragraph of "Passing Thoughts Briefly Told," the editor's personal column, informed readers, "A second Linotype is in operation this week in the *Citizen's* composing room, which should remove the bottleneck in the flow of news from the reporter and correspondent to you. George Krumsick and your editor are running the machine as time will permit and the need requires." A few weeks later readers were told that the newspaper had leased a photo engraver so that more timely photographs could be produced and a picture of the machine surrounded by the newspaper staff appeared on the front page. It wasn't revealed that the editor and his wife would be required to spend many late night hours making engravings for other area newspapers to help pay for the lease of the new engraver.

The office also had to be cleared to make room for more equipment and employees. Hundreds of individually wrapped copies of the *Christian Science Monitor* were found stacked against the wall of one office. The old editor had apparently meant to read them one day but had never gotten around to it. The *Monitors*, bales of stereotype mats and other trash had to be cleared away, and there was the chore of setting up our apartment above the newspaper. These were busy days indeed.

A recent scanning of old *Citizen* files indicates that the Missouri River played an important role in the life of the town and its citizens. There were numerous feature stories about boats and their owners, about fishing on the Missouri and Meramec rivers, including Krumsick's hunting and fishing column, which he continued to write each week, and the weekly reports of river flood stages garnered from the local office of the U.S. Army Corps of Engineers. I knew little about life on the river except for the romantic view that flowed from the pen of Mark Twain. The first week as editor I received a call to bring my camera and come down to Front Street to take a picture of an alligator gar. I had never heard of such a fish. The following day there appeared a two-column engraving on the

front page showing Krumsick and another fisher-
man holding a huge, ugly fish on a pole across their
shoulders. The caption indicated that the gar was
five feet, six inches long and weighed seventy
pounds. Many other fish stories would follow.

But the river also proved to be a dangerous and
treacherous place. It often flooded and wiped out
crops and impoverished farm families, and it
sometimes killed. A lead story on August 4 told of
the death of four Whitley siblings by drowning
after they had apparently ventured out beyond St.
John's Slough and stepped off into the deep, swift
current of the river. A front page photo focused on
the children's clothing left on the river bank. Less
than six months later, a fifth Whitley child was
drowned when her body was sucked into a storm
sewer following a downpour that flooded Washington streets.

Another river, the Meramec, was also the subject of *Citizen* attention during those months.
Krumsick often wrote of the Meramec and fishing,
the Meramec and conservation, the Meramec as a
source of beauty. When the U.S. Corps of Engineers proposed high dams on the river, citizen outrage from Krumsick and other conservationists
spilled over into public controversy. The local pastor of St. John's Gildehaus, the Rt. Rev. Msgr.
George J. Hildner, a nationally known conserva-
tionist and a persuasive voice among Catholics,

objected strongly to the multipurpose claim for the dams. The monsignor argued that the primary purpose of the dam was navigation, not recreation, conservation or flood control, as contended by proponents.

In a long editorial in the *Citizen* following a local hearing sponsored by the Chamber of Commerce, I attempted to make sense of various arguments presented at the meeting. I suggested that perhaps a better philosophy than, "Get what we can while we can get it," might be the message of the opponents, "Let's find out what we are getting before we accept it." I'm not sure if the dams were ever built on the Meramec; the argument was still raging when we sold the newspaper.

Another controversy over water, or the lack of it, dominated the news that year. It concerned a new $160,000 city reservoir under construction. The reservoir was unusual in at least two respects: First, the huge concrete structure was built above ground and, second, it wouldn't hold water—it leaked. In a front page story on May 16, readers were told that the city had taken steps to terminate the contract with the builder, Plez Lewis, and would go to court to settle payment. The following week an even larger headline stated, "City Sued for $80,744 by Plez Lewis." The story indicated that the reservoir's failure was due to engineering errors, not mistakes by the contractor. We left

Washington before the controversy was resolved.

These were a few of the big stories, but in community journalism it is news involving ordinary readers that fills most of the pages. One such segment was school news, which was challenging to cover in Washington's two high schools, one Catholic and one public, and three grammar schools—Catholic, Lutheran, and public. Students were recruited to write regular school news, but sports events needed more attention. We struck gold with Jerry Heller, a high school junior who began writing local sports and working part-time in the back shop as an apprentice. He was more interested in sports than in printing, as it turned out, but he was a bright, energetic lad. Soon his sports coverage attracted the local radio station, which offered him a slot for local sports.

After we sold the *Citizen*, Jerry studied journalism at the University of Missouri, worked at the Columbia radio station part-time while in school, and went on to pursue a career in broadcasting. At last report, he was working at station WARM in Avoca, Pennsylvania. He credits his experience on the *Citizen* with turning him on to journalism.

Looking back, the *Citizen's* editorial page seemed to be an on-again, off-again affair. I alternated between writing editorials and my personal column, but some weeks the editorial page contained neither. The old editor's hunting and fishing column was always there, along with filler items inherited from Krumsick such as "Sketches of the Misspent Life of Fred E. Ranke," which included excerpts from a book about some German prince buried in a local cemetery and a humor column entitled "Ole Uncle Fluke Says."

I first wrote under Krumsick's old personal column head, "Passing Thoughts Briefly Told," but later it became "Notes From the Editor's Scratch Pad." Krumsick continued to write conservation articles for both the *Citizen* and a couple of national publications. He observed the paper's fiftieth anniversary with a series of articles about the *Citizen's* half century of service to the community. At the age of seventy-five, Krumsick was still an active trombonist with the Washington Concert Orchestra.

One of the reasons for a lack of attention to the editorial page was the urgency of expanding advertising volume to meet mounting operating costs. The *Citizen* lagged behind the *Missourian* in circulation and it soon became clear that, if the *Citizen* was to garner its share of advertising, particularly local grocery advertising, the paper's circulation must be increased. On December 8, the *Citizen* announced that the Edwards Circulation Company of Iowa had been engaged to conduct what was called "The *Citizen's* Goodwill Subscription Campaign." Local salesmen were to be recruited to compete for $3,000 in prizes with the first place winner to receive a cash prize of $1,000.

During the next several weeks, news stories and large advertisements told of the progress of the campaign. A front page story on January 26 announced the prize winners and proclaimed that the campaign had added 1,061 new subscribers bringing the total circulation to 3,276. A full-page ad in the same edition welcomed new readers and invited advertisers "to take notice of this exciting new sales opportunity."

But the *Citizen's* increased circulation still fell below that of the *Missourian* and though advertising volume was increased as a result of the campaign so had the *Citizen's* expenses. And as the paper grew—it was now made up of two eight-page sections each week—so did the demands on Helen and me. It seemed that more and more evenings were being spent covering city council and school board meetings while Helen worked harder and harder, including long evening hours keeping the books in order, and editing and proofreading. Often as I sat listening to lengthy discussions of such public bodies with a *Missourian* reporter sitting nearby, it occurred to me that one of us was wasting his time. We were duplicating coverage of news while battling for scarce advertising dollars to pay for the news gathering.

That summer we listed the *Citizen* with a

newspaper broker and, when no out-of-town buyer was found, we agreed to a merger with the *Missourian*. When the accounts receivable were col-
lected following the sale, it was little surprise to
discover that the balance sheet indicated that our
venture into publishing showed little profit. But
we had sold the paper for more than twice what we
had paid for it just thirteen months earlier, and the
experience turned out to be a beneficial crash
course in newspaper publishing. The new publisher, who had benefited by ridding himself of a
competitor, moved the *Citizen's* publication date
to Tuesday. The last time we visited Washington, it
was still being published.

The fall of 1956 was a time of transition and
frustration for Helen and me as we searched for a
new beginning. We had sold our home on South
Lincoln Street in Salem to my parents before moving to Washington and had used the money to purchase the *Citizen*. After staying around to collect
the accounts receivable in Washington, we moved
our furniture back to Salem, stored it in the garage
of our former home, now owned by my parents,
and moved in with Helen's parents who lived next
door. One of the first opportunities for me seemed
to be active duty training at the Army Adjutant
General's School at Fort Slocum, New York, which
I took the time to apply for before we went off to
Florida for a vacation. When that didn't develop,

we explored other job opportunities before moving to Champaign later that fall where I began work as a journeyman printer for the *Daily Illini*, the student newspaper of the University of Illinois. Helen went to work at the state office of the USDA Soil Conservation Service, the same agency she had worked for in Columbia, Missouri, while I was in school.

The new jobs were challenging for a while, but within a few months we grew increasingly dissatisfied with working for others where initiative seemed only to get one into trouble, and we began looking for another newspaper to operate. We had learned a lot about publishing a community newspaper during our brief stay in Washington, we reasoned, and this time around we would pick a paper that we could edit and publish right into our golden years. It didn't turn out quite that way, but we did do a better job of choosing this second paper and our tenure was dramatically increased.

We looked over several Illinois newspaper properties before purchasing the *Arcola Record-Herald*, located just thirty miles south of Champaign. Arcola then had a population of 2,300, only about a third the size of Washington, but the paper was noncompetitive, and after our experience in Washington that fact was attractive. We learned, however, that competition from other sources can also be a problem, but at the time we didn't worry particularly about the seven other community newspapers either published or circulating in Douglas County. Arcola had other attractive features: It was located in a rich farming region, the Amish in and around nearby Arthur were a boost to tourism, and Arcola was a center for a unique industry, the manufacture, promotion, and sales of brooms made from broomcorn.

Broomcorn had once been grown throughout Central Illinois, but increasing labor costs had shifted such activity to the Southwest, particularly Oklahoma, Texas, and New Mexico. But brooms were still manufactured in Arcola and in a number of surrounding towns, including Mattoon, Charleston, and Paris. Arcola had two broom factories and was the home of the Thomas Monahan Company, a national broomcorn supplier whose warehouses dominated sites along the Illinois Central Railroad right of way. More important, the owner of the *Record-Herald* was the executive secretary of the Broom and Broomcorn Association and the editor of its weekly trade paper, the *Broom and Broomcorn News*. The contract to purchase the *Record-Herald* included an agreement for the new publisher to continue printing the *Broomcorn News* in the *Record-Herald* plant at a rate sufficient to pay off the remaining debt incurred after the down payment. That, at least, was the way it was supposed to work.

We took over publication of the *Record-Herald* the first week in July1957, and those first few months were busy as we drove back and forth to Champaign while a new house in Arco-Acres was under construction in Arcola. The old publisher, Paul A. Lindenmeyer, had maintained his office in the newspaper building pending a one-year lease agreement to be renegotiated at the end of that year. Besides editing the *Broomcorn News*, Lindenmeyer served as Douglas County chairman of the Republican Party and was involved in various oil leasing and drilling operations. Traffic to his office flowed through the *Record-Herald* newsroom, and to make things even more intolerable Lindenmeyer operated at all hours of the day and night. He also seemed to view the new publisher as a hired hand; indeed, I sat at the desk of his old editor and he operated from the same desk where he had been as the *Record-Herald* publisher for many years.

When Helen and I decided that we couldn't tolerate the arrangement any longer, we gave Lindenmeyer notice to move, which was provided for in the lease provisions, and relations deteriorated rapidly. He moved, but a few months later as the deadline for a new lease approached he made unreasonable demands for such an extension. After consulting an attorney, we bought a lot two blocks down Main Street and announced to our readers that we were constructing a new home for the *Record-Herald*, but we still had a problem.

The new building would not be completed by the time the lease ran out. As expected, on July 1, 1958, we were sued for "forcible entry and unlawful detainer" by the old publisher. The case was first heard by the local magistrate, who ruled for the newspaper but for the wrong reasons, and Lindenmeyer appealed. Meanwhile, construction of the new building continued. The case was still pending in Circuit Court in Tuscola when the building was completed and the newspaper's equipment and supplies were moved by staff members with a borrowed truck two blocks down Main Street that weekend, after the paper had been published, to its new building. A few weeks later, the townspeople turned out by the hundreds for an open house that the Lions Club, of which I had become a member, helped to promote, and the suit was dropped.

The support and assistance of George Krumsick, the old publisher of the *Washington Citizen*, had left us unprepared for the challenges we were to face with Lindenmeyer. Indeed, the lease controversy was only the first of many challenges we faced. With the building lease out of the way, we breathed a sigh of relief. It wasn't long, however, until various provisions of the printing contract for the *Broomcorn News* became points of contention.

The backshop of the *Record-Herald* was kept

busy each week after the paper was published with work on Lindenmeyer's trade paper. It seemed inevitable that things would sometimes go wrong: proofreading lapses, late delivery of proofs to Lindenmeyer's office, and so on. Such minor infractions often brought loud protests from the old publisher with threats to call in the outstanding notes we had signed under our purchase agreement, which we learned he could legally do under Illinois law. Finally, we met at the bank with our attorney in a surprise to Lindenmeyer and paid off the notes in full with a loan from the bank and from Lindenmeyer's former co-publisher, Jeff Bailey, who wanted to help insure that the young publishers had the opportunity to succeed.

A few months later when we attempted to raise the price for printing the *Broomcorn News*, Lindenmeyer balked. I still remember how depressed Helen and I were that evening as we retired thinking that we had just lost our best job-printing customer. The next morning Lindenmeyer called to invite me for a cup of coffee, an unusual occurrence. He said that he had reconsidered and wished to continue having the *News* printed at the new price on a week-to-week basis. The implication was that he might be looking elsewhere for a printer. With terms of the old contract no longer in effect, however, and with no written conditions or provisions to argue about, we printed the *News* for the next nine years without further serious disagreement. But even that didn't end the influence and competition of the old publisher upon the role of his successor.

Lindenmeyer was an ardent Republican and an active county chairman, and the *Record-Herald* under his guidance had supported Republican candidates through the years. That had worked well in the past since Douglas County was predominantly Republican. But with the influx of workers, many of them blue collar, at the huge U.S. Industrial Chemicals Company plant near Tuscola, the county seat, the Democrats began fielding stronger candidates and challenging the status quo. Democratic subscribers began showing up in the newsroom more frequently to challenge my rote editorials supporting the entire slate of Republican candidates. Such supportive editorials retained the newspaper's share of county printing, including the lucrative printing of election ballots. It didn't help the newspaper's standing with Republicans a few months later when I endorsed a Democratic candidate for county judge who surprisingly won the election. Lindenmeyer and Republican activists thought I was a traitor, but the Democrats were encouraged by the newspaper's editorial stance.

The old publisher was also an ardent sports fan, and even after selling the *Record-Herald* continued to be involved in efforts to boost sports. School news from the seven-acre campus at the edge of town, where both grade and high school buildings were a beehive of activity, was an important aspect of the paper's news coverage. And sports were taken seriously by both parents and townspeople, and by readers. The publisher was expected to cover the football games of the town's beloved Purple Riders personally. I reluctantly pursued the task, usually from the press box. I always felt that I was being challenged by the old publisher who was more often than not seen running up and down the sidelines during the game helping to keep this or that statistic for the coaching staff. At pep rallies, and at homecoming activities, there was Lindenmeyer, with obvious joy, up in front congratulating school administrators, the coaches, and the players, all of whom he seemed to know intimately.

But we not only survived the challenges provided by the old publisher during those early years; in fact, we were probably aided by his presence on the scene. In the first place, it made Helen and me strive even harder to edit the best newspaper we knew how to produce, and second, it helped to rally community support for our efforts. These benefits weren't that apparent to us at the time, but years later as I attempted to articulate the role of the community newspaper in a book I co-authored, *Electronic Age News Editing*, I better understood the dynamics of editing a weekly newspaper.

A weekly newspaper, I wrote, "is a social institution which provides the communications system needed to orient individuals toward group action and to provide social cohesion grounded in local community integration." The community press, I argued, while generally less controversial than the daily press, played an important role in providing "a means of extending prestige to hundreds of persons who, by their sheer numbers, are largely excluded from the columns of the daily press." How did the *Record-Herald* perform such a role?

The most important news a community newspaper gathers and publishes involves governmental entities. Governmental news may not be the best read, but such stories provide the information needed by readers to participate wisely in the process of governing. For ten years I covered every meeting of the Arcola City Council and Arcola School Board, which were held in the evenings and which often dragged on for hours. Meetings of the County Board of Supervisors, which were held during the day, had to be covered indirectly.

The political aspects of governing were more interesting to report and often more controversial. Sometimes state and federal candidates visited Arcola, but most of the coverage was of local candidates and officials. In many respects, the late Tip O'Neill, speaker of the U.S. House of Representatives, was correct. "All politics is local." It was certainly a good local story when a congressional candidate visited your town. I remember also covering a speech by Richard Nixon when he was running for president and visited in nearby Sullivan, but the most significant story I wrote involving a national political figure was a story about local reaction to the assassination of President John F. Kennedy with a picture of the American flag flying at half staff above the local post office.

By sheer volume, news about school activities dominated the editorial columns of the *Record-Herald*. Each week during the months the schools were in session, the paper published an ArcoLite section of school news gathered and edited by students under the direction of an English teacher. Another English teacher, Mildred Dennis, wrote a weekly column, "Just Wondering," which was one of the best read features in the paper. The Arcola school band and its booster club often received individual coverage. But sports activities were the most frequent sources of stories: football, basketball, track. Both football and basketball coverage was supported by full page advertisements that appeared the week of home games under the sponsorship of more than a hundred local merchants and professional people.

Basketball was the most demanding sport to cover because there were so many games and tournaments. A backshop employee with a knack for writing who wanted to make a little extra money was generally assigned to cover the home games. When a picture was required, I generally showed up with my Speed Graphic or Rollei to take a shot of the tourney winner posing with a trophy. This was during the years when all high schools competed against one another before they were divided according to enrollment. Twice during the decade we published the paper, the Arcola Purple Riders were in the so-called Sweet Sixteen and played in first-round supersectional games.

I remember best the 1964 supersectional in Horton Fieldhouse at Illinois State University in Normal when the Purple Riders played the Reds of Stephen Decatur. The Fieldhouse seated 7,000, and it was filled with noisy fans. The Riders were defeated 53 to 37, knocking out their chance of competing as an Elite Eight team in Champaign, but it had been a glorious year for the Riders. When the Appleknockers of Cobden came through Arcola on their way to Champaign the following day, members of the Riders team boarded the Illinois Central passenger train when it stopped in Arcola to cheer on a small town team that had made it to the Elite Eight. The Arcola superintendent, Leon Sitter, a native of Cobden, had arranged for the two teams to meet. I got on the train and was so busy taking pictures that I failed to hear the warning that the train was pulling out of the station. Helen dutifully retrieved me later when the train stopped at Tuscola seven miles to the north.

Much of the local news was about efforts for community betterment or more social pleasure as people joined together in clubs and organizations such as the Chamber of Commerce, the Lions Club, or various Masonic groups. A church page listed the various weekly services and provided for a weekly "Pastor's Corner" shared by local ministers. A section entitled "Peekin' Thru the Keyhole" included social news of comings and goings. Agricultural news was presented through the Farm Adviser's column, feature stories by D. N. Roberts, a part-time farm editor, and reports about new research, the weather, and crop yields. Historical features appeared from time to time by Frank F. Collins, a long time editor and publisher of the *Record-Herald* then living in Champaign. Mildred Dennis, in addition to her weekly "Just Wondering" column, wrote occasional features about old houses and local residents involved in interesting events or activities.

Promotion of community events and business campaigns often ended up in the news columns. The *Record-Herald* sponsored the annual Miss

Arcola Beauty Contest to select a queen to compete in the Moultrie-Douglas County Fair each summer. The county fair winner advanced to the state contest held in Springfield each January where a Miss Illinois Fair Queen was named. There were promotion stories about the Little Theatre in nearby Sullivan, the only such professional thespian group at that time between Chicago and St. Louis. Retail business promotions often found their way into the news columns as well. Other stories promoted local industry: the broom suppliers and manufacturers; and Collegiate Cap and Gown where some seventy-five employees, most of them women, made academic and religious caps and gowns for rent and sale through the Champaign headquarters. The line between news and advertising was often less distinct in the community than in the urban press. The *Record-Herald* even ran some reader ads on the front page during those years.

Periodically, there were stories of storms and natural disasters and how the community dealt with them. Stories sometimes dealt with unusual aspects of community life and events: the Raggedy Ann doll created by John B. Gruelle, an Arcola native; the development of Rockome Gardens, a growing tourist attraction west of town; and the titles of books donated in the memorial book promotion at the Arcola Public Library. Then there were the vital statistics garnered from the court-house and the nearby Tuscola hospital: who was born, who had applied for a license to wed, and who had died.

"The Editor's Scratch Pad," the editor's personal column, appeared in the upper left-hand corner of the front page each week. It often was the last thing written before press time Wednesday noon. Sometimes it treated a single issue or topic, but more often it dealt with several topics reported in the news that week, which the editor wanted to enlarge upon, interpret, or explain. More often than not, the column provided the only editorial comment in the paper; there simply wasn't the time nor the resources to produce a full-blown editorial page each week—though this occasionally happened. The editor's column was probably the best read feature in the paper, but the opinions expressed there could produce controversy. Often letters to the editor, published elsewhere in the newspaper, disagreed with the editor's point of view, but the forum was open to comment on any topic of public interest as long as it wasn't obscene or libelous.

As the volume of news and advertising copy grew through the years, Helen and I were increasingly faced with a number of problems common to most community editors at that time: a lack of time to do as good a job as we would have liked to do and frustration over demands on our time by the public, the lack of an adequate staff to provide the needed division of labor, and a related problem—an inadequate financial base, specifically a lack of advertising revenue. Years later in research for *Electronic Age News Editing*, a book I co-authored, I was surprised by the commonality of responses from some sixty community editors in regard to these three problems. At the *Record-Herald*, the front office staff included only two part-time employees in addition to Helen and me. In the backshop, there were four, sometimes five, full-time employees and two or three part-time apprentices. There was work for additional hands but insufficient funds to hire them.

Our daily routine during the ten years in Arcola varied little from week to week. I generally made the rounds in Arcola to sell advertising and gather news on Monday and part of the day on Tuesday, with a run to Tuscola, the county seat, wedged in somewhere to make contact with various county offices at the courthouse for news and printing orders. Helen, in addition to being the "brunette who ran the office"—she was listed as co-publisher on the editorial masthead—called on advertisers in Mattoon on Monday, read galley and page proofs, supervised the society editor and other part-time help, waited on customers in the front office, and punched tape on the Teletypesetter in her spare time. She also maintained the records and tended to most of the correspondence and billing of customers, very often during long evening hours or on weekends. When emergency surgery laid her up for six weeks, her desk was overflowing with paperwork piled there by me and others awaiting her return. I explained to readers how much we all missed the brunette who ran the office in a boldface paragraph in "Notes From the Editor's Scratch Pad."

After the *Record-Herald* was published each Wednesday afternoon, I usually deserted Helen, put on my printer's apron, and went to the back-shop where work was underway on the *Broomcorn News* and other job printing orders. As a journeyman printer, I knew how to do most of the printing operations, and, unfortunately, I was the best machinist the paper had and the two Linotypes, one with Teletypesetter capabilities, demanded frequent maintenance and repair. In addition, much of my time was spent training apprentices only to see them leave for other more lucrative jobs once they had learned the printing trade. And during the Vietnam War years, we lost three apprentices and printers to the draft.

My teaching resume, my curriculum vitae, later listed ten years as a publisher in Arcola. I remember an administrator at Ole Miss asked me when I was interviewing there for a teaching position if I had actually had ten years of experience or if I had one year of experience repeated ten times. I wasn't ready then to acknowledge that his assessment had merit, but looking back the publishing connection in Arcola had indeed become more and more repetitive with each passing year.

Repetitive or not, the operation was profitable enough that we were able to modernize the production plant through the years: A new photoengraver was leased to make possible more timely pictures, first one and later a second automatic job press was purchased to keep up with printing orders, a Teletypesetter was acquired to speed up the composition of news stories, and finally, an expensive Ludlow was purchased, which simplified the composition of display type. But in the end, this state-of-the-art equipment only increased the workload without producing the extra profits needed to hire additional employees. Finally, we realized we were creating yet another problem: We were investing too much money in a community newspaper in a small town—Arcola—and might never be able to sever our publishing connection without financial loss.

In the end, it was probably "burn out" that brought us to the decision to sell the *Record-Herald*, though I don't recall that the term was then in vogue. After ten years without a vacation and facing the prospect of more of the same, Helen and I just grew weary of what had been an exciting adventure in publishing. Indeed, the role of a community newspaper editor and publisher is an important and satisfying position in many respects though it is often little appreciated by the majority of residents and business leaders. The wall of the *Record-Herald* newsroom was covered with plaques and certificates the paper had won through the years in the Illinois Press Association's Best Newspaper Contests, including first place in the general excellence category for the last three years. But editorial excellence doesn't necessarily translate into financial success. Indeed, extended news coverage only adds to the overall cost of publication; it takes increased advertising lineage to ensure financial success, and that base seemed to be shrinking.

We listed the *Record-Herald* for sale with a broker several months before we were successful in finding a suitable buyer. He was Lewis (Dick) Williams, who for twenty years had served in various editorial capacities with the *Chicago Tribune* and who recently had come off a publishing venture in Tucson, Arizona, which had gone sour. The deal was completed in less than a week and the new publisher took over publication on July 1, 1967, just ten years to the day after Helen and I had assumed such responsibilities. In contrast to our sale of the *Washington Citizen*, this time around we knew what we wanted to do next, and my plans to teach journalism while working on a doctoral degree were formalized while Helen and I were still involved with helping the new publisher take over the operation of the paper.

While the *Record-Herald* sale marked the end to newspaper publishing for Helen and me, the experience had a profound effect on us and many happy memories have survived despite all the frustration and hard work. We still receive a complimentary copy of the paper each week with each succeeding publisher—there have been three of them—retaining our name on the subscription list.

The large, framed charcoal drawing of Abe Lincoln that once hung prominently above my desk in the *Record-Herald* newsroom—a gift from Helen's mother—now hangs over my filing cabinets and and other office equipment stored in our garage. One vivid memory I have of the newspaper office, Beverly, if you are still following these reminiscences, is of you sitting at my desk below that Lincoln picture as a schoolgirl helping your uncle and aunt put out the newspaper. Your summer visits were a joy to both of us. Looking back, Helen and I also take some satisfaction in the fact that the *Record-Herald* has survived through all these years, although we did not.

The Academic Connection

I suppose it was inevitable that I would one day be attracted to teaching. Despite my shyness, I had entertained the notion of jumping from the newsroom to the classroom even before Helen and I had purchased the *Arcola Record-Herald* in 1957. Dr. Howard R. Long, a former Missouri weekly newspaper publisher and then chairman of the Department of Journalism at Southern Illinois University at Carbondale, had encouraged me to become a teacher but had warned that a prerequisite was study toward a doctoral degree. That suggestion was reinforced some time later during an interview with Fred S. Siebert, dean of the College of Communications at the University of Illinois, while I was working at the *Daily Illini*, the student newspaper. A master's degree, which I received at Missouri, was simply not sufficient to gain a continuing appointment at most accredited schools or departments of journalism.

When the deal was being closed to sell the *Record-Herald* in 1967, however, I took up the idea of teaching once again and wrote to graduate schools at the University of Missouri, the University of Illinois, and Southern Illinois University at Carbondale inquiring about the requirements of graduate study and the financial assistance that might be available. Within a few days, and weeks before receiving responses from the other two institutions, Dr. Long called me at the newspaper to answer my queries. Helen and I, still busy with assisting the new owners of the *Record-Herald* to take over, began seriously considering moving to Carbondale. But there was another important consideration on both our minds, and that was getting away from it all for a much needed vacation.

Helen finished with closing out her accounts receivable by August 1 but, because of a shortage of help, I continued for a couple of weeks assisting the new publishers in the backshop. On August 26, we finally packed the Thunderbird and left for a planned 9,000-mile, thirty-day tour across the West, then on to Alaska by way of Prince Rupert and the Inland Waterway Ferry, returning by the Alaska Highway across Canada. That was the vacation I wanted to take. Upon our return, we rested up for a few days, did the laundry, caught up on our mail, then flew to Hawaii for ten days to tour the Islands. That was the vacation Helen wanted to take. Returning home in November, we got serious about plans to move to Carbondale.

The first week of December we moved into our

new house on Canterbury Drive, spent most of the month getting organized and, on January 2, the beginning of the winter quarter, I became a doctoral student at SIUC. I also began a teaching assistantship in the Department of Journalism, working with reporting students in the newsroom of the *Daily Egyptian*, the student newspaper. The half-time assistantship required twenty hours of work a week and paid $260 a month, which later was raised to $295. There was no G.I. Bill to boost my support, but the assistantship did call for a tuition waiver.

After a few weeks at home, Helen became bored and went to work, first at the USDA Farmers Home Administration office in Murphysboro and later with the *Illinois Baptist*, a denominational weekly newspaper published in Carbondale with a circulation of 52,000 throughout Illinois. She also served without pay as a proofreader and typist for my various writing projects, both as a student and later as a teacher. Those first three years were both busy and hectic, but they were satisfying also as progress was made toward that elusive graduate degree needed for me to become a full-fledged journalism faculty member.

I recently ran across a mimeographed copy of the degree requirements issued to me as I began course work toward that Doctor of Philosophy degree, and I am surprised with the simplicity of the statement: "The Ph.D. degree is awarded for high accomplishment in a particular discipline or a recognized interdisciplinary area, as measured by the student's ability to pass the preliminary examination for admission to candidacy, meet the research tool requirement of the program, perform a piece of original research, present the results in proper form in a dissertation, and defend the dissertation before a faculty committee." It sounded so doable, but for a guy who was about to turn fifty and hadn't been in a classroom for fifteen years it took a few adjustments and much hard work.

At that time, a doctoral student majoring in journalism was required to have two minor areas of study outside the school. Mine were English, where I pursued American literature, and political science, which was then called government. Two research tools were also required: Mine were Spanish and statistics. I had studied Spanish as a pre-journalism requirement at the University of Missouri, but I found, regretfully, that I had forgotten most of it. Statistics was viewed as a necessary tool by my graduate adviser, but it had been thirty years since I had studied high school algebra. It took much individual study to become refreshed about the relationship of terms in the equations my statistics teacher wrote on the blackboard. The Spanish requirement was met by passing the so-called Princeton test, which became an insurmountable hurdle for some graduate students. I passed it after taking a noncredit refresher class offered for graduate students. Statistics I found fascinating because, as I was to learn, it had less to do with mathematics, which I had never studied at the college level, than with describing and analyzing an array of numbers.

My dissertation, which was completed and defended in July 1971, entitled "An Analysis of Views Concerning Press Performance," was a quantitative (statistical) research study involving a purposive sample of 150 subjects drawn from seven communities in Southern Illinois and Southeastern Missouri. Five occupational role categories made up the subgroups of the sample: newsmen, politicians, businessmen, professionals, and blue collar workers. The study, which explored the growing diversity of views and attitudes newspaper critics express toward press performance, may not have uncovered anything startling from the point of view of working journalists, but it did sufficiently impress my committee of five educators, two from outside the School of Journalism, who recommended that my dissertation be accepted "toward partial fulfillment of the requirements for the Degree of Doctor of Philosophy."

Looking back after more than twenty years, I still remember the challenges posed by many of my classes and the excellent teachers, some with whom I was associated years later on thesis and dissertation committees of students working under my guidance. And I have many satisfying memories of my work as a teaching assistant in journalism, mostly out of the newsroom of the campus newspaper then published in a frame building adjacent to the old Army barracks, which served as housing for the Journalism Department offices, labs, and for faculty. The system of examinations graduate students faced, however, was often frustrating, unduly time consuming, and sometimes patently unfair.

At that time many graduate programs required an examination to determine if the candidate could be expected to successfully complete such a course of study. At SIUC the exam was given, not before the student entered the program, but sometime during the first year of study. Strangely, doctoral students took the same exam as master's degree students were required to take upon completing their course work. In other words, doctoral students were examined over material they would be studying, which tended to impress upon them how much they didn't yet know. It probably did little, however, to measure their ability to pursue such a program of study. It also allowed a faculty member to require beginning doctoral students to do remedial work to make up for any perceived shortcomings in their preparation for graduate study. I still resent a ten-page paper required of seven of us from one graduate faculty member who didn't like our responses to his question: "What is a theory, and how does one go about developing a theory?" I later discovered the answer he was looking for in a textbook he used in one of his seminars.

But the mother of all examinations must have been the twenty-hour series of exams scattered over five evenings that constituted the doctoral preliminary examination. Exams given through the years by various faculty members were then available (albeit unofficially) to guide students in their preparation, but the questions tended to cover the universe. In addition to a review of course materials, other reading went into study for the exams. For a government professor's exam, I read thirty books from a list he supplied. One student told me he felt like a sieve as he kept feeding more and more information into his system while realizing that much of it kept running out in the process.

I still remember those four-hour sessions at the typewriter with nothing but paper for typing and a pencil for editing. Even a dictionary, which might have come in handy on an occasion or two to determine what a question even meant, was forbidden. In most of my sessions I produced twelve to fifteen pages of double-spaced copy, but it wasn't particularly comforting when another doctoral candidate beside me, who could type faster than I could think, was producing twenty or more pages during the same period. Luckily, our responses were not evaluated on the basis of volume.

A few days later, we were faced with the oral portion of the "prelims," a two-hour session with the five-member committee in which students had the opportunity either to lift themselves from any traps they may have fallen into, or to dig themselves even deeper into that hole. Adding to the challenge, the oral questions were not confined to the student's responses on the written exam, providing the faculty member an opportunity to put a student in his or her place should the student exercise too much independence. The system tended to train one to leap hurdle after hurdle and to award patience and endurance, if not scholarship and intelligence. I managed to get over the hurdles, but a few did not, which served to raise the level of anxiety for other graduate students still in the process.

By the time I was granted the Ph.D. degree, I was teaching full time as an instructor. Two things happened almost immediately upon receiving the doctorate: first, my status as instructor, which was a term appointment, was elevated to assistant professor—which was a continuing appointment—and my students began calling me "Doctor." The appointment change was good; it meant that I had a job if I wanted to remain at SIUC. At least I had a job until the matter of tenure was considered; but more on that later. The title was a different matter.

Faculty members seemed to encourage use of the title "Doctor," as any doctoral granting institution might be expected to do, and the students followed along, especially when they wanted to appear deferential. I was always uncomfortable with such a title, which in the real world is generally reserved for the medical doctor, who as one colleague put it, "drives a Mercedes, winters in Bermuda, and plays golf at courses with real sand in the traps." About the best an academic doctor can do, according to my colleague, "is evoke the interest, if not the adoration, of the students in the front row of his classes, many of them in the late stages of recovery from facial blemishes." At any rate, for the next fifteen years I became Doctor Stonecipher to a generation of journalism students at SIUC despite the vocational deception, and even in retirement a few of my more deferential students still make such references when we meet.

I had always assumed that when I faced a class of journalism students I would be lecturing to them about various aspects of community journalism. That was my area of expertise, if that isn't being too boastful; the doctorate was viewed as something added—a sort of union card—to better secure my continuing employment as a college teacher. But in the fall of 1969 when the director of the School of Journalism (the department had been upgraded to a school and a new wing of the Communications Building was under construction across campus at the time to house it) approached me about teaching full time while I completed my degree, he had three courses that needed an instructor: "Writing for the Mass Media," "Editorial Writing," and "The Law of Journalism." The first was the beginning writing course for news-editorial majors and posed no problem for me because it did relate to community journalism; the second, editorial writing, was an advanced skills course not generally taught by a new teacher; and the law course was perceived as one of the most difficult courses in the curriculum to teach.

My first response to the director's offer was hesitation; I had expressed an interest in gaining experience as a classroom teacher before completing my degree, but not a full-time position and not in a specialized course such as "The Law of Journalism." The director encouraged me—after all, it was August and he needed someone to meet three classes in September—and I finally said "yes" after much self doubt and trepidation. The director had made the offer seem more of a challenge—an offer I couldn't refuse. Looking back, I'm thankful that I mustered up the courage to accept the appointment despite the hard work and frustration of that first year of teaching while completing my doctoral studies. But I've never fully forgiven the director who, for his own reasons, never fully informed me about what I was getting into.

During the break between summer school and the beginning of the fall quarter, I put aside all work toward the doctorate and began preparing for those three classes I would be facing in just a couple of weeks. The two writing courses were manageable, but the law course proved to be even more complex than I had any reason to expect. I had studied constitutional law, and one segment of that course dealt with First Amendment cases, but the new 800-page textbook, which had already been adopted and ordered for students, was filled with scores of cases, mostly U.S. Supreme Court cases, in some areas where I had little knowledge: libel, privacy, pornography, free press and fair trial, journalistic privilege, access to governmental bodies and records, commercial speech, antitrust laws, and copyright. I hastily prepared abstracts and briefs for the law course and began organizing lectures and updating syllabi for all three courses. There wasn't much time and, as the opening of school approached, what had seemed to be a challenge now appeared to be more like the approach of an academic doomsday.

Looking back, the assignment of those three courses was to define my teaching and research interests throughout my academic career in a way I little suspected. Indeed, I taught those same three courses at least once each academic year for the next fifteen years, and I did research and was published in scholarly journals in two of those subject areas. The one section of "Writing for the Mass Media" eventually became a twice-a-week lecture to four sections with a combined enrollment of up to eighty students with labs conducted by graduate assistants, who I supervised. And the course later served an important gatekeeper function, screening out many students who lacked the language skills to pursue journalism as a major.

The editorial writing class, which later became "Critical and Persuasive Writing," was limited to twenty students and afforded a seminar approach to teaching and a departure from the norm in most undergraduate classes. The class also gave students the opportunity to be published in the campus newspaper, the *Daily Egyptian*, with weekly assignments to produce various forms of persuasive writing—editorials, opinion columns, critical reviews—submitted for publication if considered worthy by the editor. An interest in broadening the scope of the course led to my participation in the National Conference of Editorial Writers for ten years and eventually to producing a textbook, *Editorial and Persuasive Writing*, published in 1979 by Hastings House of New York. A second edition of the text, published in 1990, is still used by a few schools, but persuasive writing courses have recently fallen into disfavor in many schools.

It was the assignment to teach press law, however, that proved to be the most influential in determining the direction and scope of a major portion of my future scholarly activities. "The Law of Journalism" was a senior level course required of all news-editorial majors and open to graduate students as well. It was offered each semester and, during the regular school year, generally attracted forty to fifty students and half that number during the summer term. It was a challenging course to teach with additional cases being rendered by the courts each year and with numerous changes in the statutes and regulations of interest to the press. It was also a difficult course for many students who had been attracted to journalism because of an aptitude for writing, not legal analysis.

The law class proved to be interesting, however, and it was not difficult for the teacher to demonstrate that what was being studied had meaning in the world outside the classroom. Invited guests— the state's attorney, a circuit judge, journalists who had become defendants in a libel or privacy case— helped to heighten student interest. When the SIUC Law School was established, a sprinkling of law students drifted into the class, generally two or three a semester, which helped to broaden the legal horizons of class members. And, ironically perhaps, the course in press law is the course most graduates refer to when we meet after they have left campus and are working at the trade.

Teaching the law class also led to my exploration of legal research with the establishment of the law library on campus. Later, with assistance from a faculty colleague with an interest in law, a seminar in legal and governmental research methods was established for our graduate students. It also led to a book, *The Mass Media and the Law in Illinois*, published by the Southern Illinois University Press in 1976, which is still in print but badly in need of revision. Indeed, that faculty member, Dr. Robert Trager, and I went on to research and write numerous legal papers and co-authored articles published in *Journalism Quarterly*, the official journal of journalism educators, and in various law reviews and professional journals. Such research and publication helped to make possible merit pay increase, tenure, and promotion through the years. Like it or not, the publish or perish syndrome was and still is very much alive at SIUC. For Dr. Trager it led to a law degree a few years later from Stanford University, but after practicing law for a few years he returned to teaching journalism and pursuing legal research at the University of Colorado.

But back to the beginning, I still remember the frustration of that first year of teaching. In so many ways, I was unprepared for the undertaking. I had lectured some in the Army and had worked in Sunday School before that, even served as Sunday School superintendent for a short time, but I had never taught a class of college students. As a journalism instructor I only had to face classes ten or twelve hours a week, but I learned that preparing for all those lectures was very time consuming. Grading all the written work coming out of the classes was even more time consuming. I also learned that even a new teacher has other duties on school and college committees and is often required to engage in academic functions across campus. And that first year I still had three doctoral level courses to take and a dissertation to launch.

I suppose that at age fifty-two students saw me as more of an authority figure than had I been the age of most beginning teachers, but that didn't help much when one's mouth would suddenly get dry during a lecture without warning and one had to keep going knowing that the dryness would eventually pass. I suppose that the inspiration of former teachers who I most admired helped to keep me going. An effective teacher, educational psychologists say, is one who holds up high expectations that his or her students will succeed. I could relate to that.

Two University of Missouri professors, Frank Luther Mott, who was dean emeritus when I sat in his classes, and Dean Earl English, were excellent role models for their teaching skills as well as having something challenging to say. And my constitutional law professor at SIUC, Dr. Randall Nelson, who was blind but who was more discerning than any sighted teacher I have ever known, was an inspiration to me and a generation of journalism students. And he certainly demonstrated that he expected his students to learn. But eventually it was a deep desire to teach and learn that kept me going, battling my shyness and other obstacles every step of the way.

That first year of teaching came during the height of campus unrest and student protests over the war in Vietnam. Some demonstrations against expansion of the war with the bombings of Cambodia and the continuation of the drafting of Americans to fight in that war turned to violence. On the SIUC campus, the focus of much of the protest was a Vietnamese Study Center in Woody Hall, which students believed was financed by the CIA, and the center for ROTC training in Anthony Hall. But anyone viewed as being in a position of authority, particularly a university administrator, was likely to be the target of such protests.

During the spring quarter of 1970, an escalation of violence brought a contingent of the Illinois National Guard under the command of brother Amos, who was then a colonel, along with scores of Illinois State Police to campus, which seemed to further fuel the violence. One particularly violent evening in which some 3,000 students and others staged a sit-in at the downtown intersection of Main Street and Illinois Avenue and the blockage of the nearby Illinois Central Railroad brought destruction to scores of retail businesses after police used tear gas to break up the sit-in. Helen and I were caught in the gas as we visited the near-by post office. Hardly a plate glass window escaped the carnage as the protesters were driven back toward the campus.

A few days later the tragic killing of four students by the National Guard on the Kent State campus in Ohio further escalated protests against the war. Eventually the SIUC campus was closed for the remainder of the quarter and a 6 p.m. curfew was put into place throughout Carbondale. Teachers were instructed to give all students a satisfactory mark for the courses they never had the opportunity to complete. And perhaps it was just as well because there wasn't much learning going on in the classroom.

A college teacher's performance at SIUC, and at most other large universities, is measured at three levels: ability as a classroom teacher, academic scholarship as demonstrated through research and publication, and professional service, which in the case of a journalism teacher meant participation in and contributions made to professional organizations affiliated with the mass media. For a faculty member in a continuing appointment, both tenure and promotion were based on performance in these three areas. Teaching performance relied heavily on one's Instructor and Course Evaluation (ICE) Reports, then a fifty-six-item computerized evaluation completed by students near the end of the course.

The ICE computer printout showed the mean received on each item plus the decile the teacher fell into at the department, college, and university level of all courses evaluated across campus. There were additional computations grouping items in subject categories such as personal and impersonal characteristics of the instructor, course structuring by the instructor, course quality, course difficulty, items measuring progress on objectives, and items classified as "student self ratings." If the teacher's ICE evaluations weren't considered satisfactory, tenure or promotion papers generally never went forward. The same was true of professional service, which one either had or didn't have.

It was the demonstration of academic scholarship that proved most difficult to establish sufficiently to satisfy reviewing committees at various higher administrative levels. The problem often arose first in the process for establishing tenure, the granting of job security for teachers, which has

become a point of controversy and at times litiga-
tion in the federal courts following a denial action
by the university.

There was no problem for me in gaining
tenure, but that was true largely because research
and publication wasn't viewed with the same
importance as it was to be later. Indeed, of the first
five faculty members I had the opportunity to vote
on favorably for tenure after I became a member of
the tenured faculty, four were ultimately denied
tenure by higher administrative committees. Such
faculty members received notice that their contracts would be terminated at the end of a set time,
generally at the end of the following academic year.
It wasn't until I was caught up in the evaluation
process of determining which faculty member
should be retained—tenured and eventually promoted—and which should be dismissed that I
became troubled with the goals of journalism education and the process of reaching those goals.

Part of the problem was that, while a journalism faculty must have sufficient professional experience to teach the skills courses and to meet the
requirements of an accredited program, the reward
system at SIUC was so constructed that it encouraged academic scholarship through research and
publication, not teaching and professional service,
once such faculty members were under contract.
The new faculty member with a doctorate and a

newly acquired research tool often was better equipped to meet the requirements for tenure and promotion than the person joining the faculty with a professional background, no matter how important such media experience may be for the retention of accreditation for the school.

I was faced with such a dilemma. The professional experience that helped me obtain my faculty status little prepared me for the research I was expected to do. My doctorate and my two research tools, Spanish and statistics, didn't match with my teaching assignment or my research interests. It took much self-study and experimentation to gain the expertise in legal research that did relate to my teaching efforts and was a tool not available to me when I was working toward my doctorate. As the result of such a delay, it took six years and a second attempt to move from assistant professor to associate professor and another five years to be promoted to full professor.

Three books, two of them co-authored, more than a dozen scholarly papers, and a long list of publications, most of them published in refereed journals, along with half a dozen chapters or articles in books edited by others, were the key to such promotions. Teaching alone, not even skilled teaching with extensive professional service, was enough to survive.

Looking back, my research and publication,

without doubt, improved my teaching efforts because much of it was directly related to the subject matter of my assigned courses. But the emphasis on research can result in time taken away from a faculty member's teaching effort and his or her availability to students. Recent criticism by professional groups has brought calls for revamping journalism education by refocusing the faculty's attention on teaching rather than on research. The answer, of course, is a balance between the needed professional experience for teaching the skills courses and the academic scholarship, gained largely through continuing research and publication, with the goal of educating students to think critically and analytically and to acquire the skills needed to express themselves through written, oral, and visual modes of communication.

It's difficult to justify the process of tenure and promotion in terms of the primary goal of a university to educate individual students to think critically and analytically and to instill in them a knowledge, appreciation, and understanding of the diversity of human experience and culture. My experience was that hours and hours of effort must often go into collecting the documentation needed to justify such rewards to members of a committee across campus, most of whom had never met you or knew anything of your teaching skills or academic scholarship other than information obtained from the file. Thus, such files become quite voluminous by the time they reach their destination.

By the time I was recommended for promotion to full professor in 1981, however, I had come to view teaching as a rewarding profession that allowed one to pursue scholarly activities uninterrupted and sometimes to discover things few others knew, and the opportunity to make such information available to students in classes. A scholar's most substantial reward, Oliver Wendell Holmes, Jr., once said, is "the secret isolated joy of the thinker, who knows that, a hundred years after he is dead and forgotten, men who have never heard of him will be moving to the measure of his thought." But there are other more immediate joys in teaching. I remember the pride and elation of showing off a copy of my first book to faculty colleagues and the joy of seeing my byline on an article in *Journalism Quarterly* or in a law review, no matter how frequently it may occur.

There is also a joy, at least on one's better days at the lectern, to share knowledge with a classroom full of students, and finding most of them interested in what you are saying. But I learned that it's probably too much to hope that all are listening or that even those who are will always be interested despite your best efforts to hold up high expectations for their success. I recall that my mother, then in her eighties, attended one of my classes to hear me lecture. It was the large writing class that met in Lawson Hall with its elevated seats arranged in a half-circular fashion and a table running in front of the chairs. Helen accompanied her, and they sat together in the front row in the seats of absent class members. I thought I had done a pretty good job of lecturing that day, but when I got no reaction from my mother afterward, I asked her what she thought about the class. I expected her to be impressed by the state-of-the-art classroom with its automatic screens, overhead projector, and maybe even of her son, the instructor. But she commented, "There were two or three students up in the back row who weren't paying any attention to what you were saying."

It may have been mom's first university class, but she had been quick to put her finger on a basic communications problem: Messages, no matter how carefully presented, are not always received by their intended target. There was another problem with teaching "Writing for the Mass Media" and that was that almost half the students enrolled in the course had deficiencies in language skills as measured by a standardized test administered each semester. These skills had to be corrected before the student was allowed to advance into other journalism courses. This firm approach by the teacher didn't help his student evaluations, particularly on the ICE's personal-interpersonal items such as "encouraged student participation."

Student responses suggested that maybe there was too much of a first sergeant mentality entering the classroom from the instructor's past. In the promotion file submitted in 1981 for full professor, one of my former students, then the managing editor of the *Jacksonville* (Florida) *Journal*, wrote in a letter recommending promotion, "While Dr. Stonecipher may not offer the pizzazz of some teachers, he does offer something more important: He knows what he's talking about. And students know that." In retrospect, I'm sure I could have used a little more pizzazz, but it's reassuring to know that at least one former student thought I knew what I was talking about and was willing to put it into writing.

I did come to feel I knew what I was talking about as I gained experience in a wide range of scholarly activities. Through the years I taught seven different courses, including three graduate seminars. I headed the news-editorial sequence for ten years, working closely with new faculty members teaching skills courses. I was deputy director of the School of Journalism for four years, filling in for the director when he was off campus. But the most satisfying and lasting aspect of teaching, it turns out, was working with graduate students in seminars, in the classroom as teaching assistants, and through my participation on some sixty thesis and dissertation committees, chairing some fifteen doctoral committees. Most of those doctoral students now teach at colleges and universities, some heading departments and schools of journalism.

Among those who became journalism administrators are Douglas Anderson, director of the Walter Cronkite School of Journalism and Telecommunication at Arizona State University; David Reed, chair of the Department of Journalism, Eastern Illinois University; Don Sneed, chair of the Department of Journalism, University of Mississippi; and Douglas Tarpley, chair of the School of Journalism, Regent University, Virginia Beach, Virginia. Donna Dickerson, who served as my teaching assistant while working on her doctorate, is now the director of the School of Mass Communication, University of South Florida. Another former teaching assistant, Ferrell Ervin, is now chair of the Department of Mass Communication, Southeast Missouri State University. And Sherrie Good, a long-time teaching assistant who taught for a couple of years at Sangamon State University, Springfield, Illinois, after receiving her doctorate at SIUC is the executive editor in charge of a string of ten community newspapers published by the *Orange County Register* in California.

Among former doctoral students under my supervision who went on to teach journalism are William Babcock, now at the University of Minnesota; Jean Barres, Baylor University at Waco, Texas; George Johnson, James Madison University, Harrisonburg, Virginia; George Killenberg, University of South Florida; Achal Mehra, Albright College, Reading, Pennsylvania; Thomas Schwartz, Ohio State University; and Michael Sherer, University of Nebraska at Omaha. Ruth Eshenaur, who accepted a position as a teaching missionary in Nairobi, Africa, after receiving her doctorate, broke off communications with her former mentor after a few months and, like Dr. Livingston, disappeared into darkest Africa.

One of the best and the brightest of my former students, however, and one of the hardest working, was Kyu Ho Youm, now an associate professor of journalism at Arizona State University. Helen and I visited Dr. Youm last year in Tempe and were dinner guests in the family's new home in Phoenix. Special guests that evening were my favorite niece, Beverly, and her family, who had entertained us all on a previous visit at her home in Paradise Valley. We talked of academic pursuits, the status of health care, and how to survive in the desert Southwest. Helen and I especially enjoyed playing the role once again of American grandparents to the Youm boys—Harry and Eugene. We visited with Dr. Youm more recently in Atlanta, Georgia, where we were attending the annual conference of the AEJMC. He had just returned to the United States after spending a month in South Korea where he was doing research for a book on Korean press law, returning home by way of Australia where he presented three legal papers at a scholarly conference. What boundless energy these young people demonstrate!

I'm reminded that one of the problems in teaching is that students, particularly undergraduates, remain the same age while the teacher grows older. Most of the students in my classes were twenty-one or twenty-two, and in those same classes year after year the students remained the same age. But the teacher was growing older and older.

Yet another problem with teaching journalism is keeping up with the rapidly changing technology of communications. During my lifetime, print media have gone from the laborious process of handsetting type to the mechanical Linotype and, more recently, to electronic typesetting. The reporter has progressed from pencil and note pad to the typewriter and now to the computer. Too long out of the newsroom and the journalism teacher begins to feel that the technology of his craft has left him behind.

After fifteen years of teaching and just a few weeks short of my sixty-sixth birthday, I retired at the end of the summer term in 1984. Helen retired from her job as area clerk with the USDA Soil Conservation Service at the same time, though retirement doesn't seem an appropriate term for what has followed, but more on that later. As it turned out, the academic connection was not entirely severed even after becoming an annuitant of the State Universities Retirement System. And life off campus has continued, if at a slower pace.

Professor Kyu Ho Youm of Arizona State University, read an early draft of this manuscript and noted several typographical errors and grammatical glitches, for which I am thankful, and had a recommendation regarding this academic chapter.

"You might note," he wrote, "the enormous impact you have had on the First Amendment Scholarship through your SIUC graduate students. I still remember the *Journalism Quarterly* footnote naming you one of five or six most influential First Amendment scholars by nurturing Ph.D. students in media law. Your first-rate scholarship and teaching, I think, deserve to be noted in your book and the fact that JQ, the most prestigious research journal in our field, recognized your distinguished contributions to First Amendment research over the years."

Modesty, of course, prevents me from making any such broad-based scholastic claim for myself, but, ironically, I find much satisfaction in the fact that one of my former doctoral students would make such a suggestion.

The Religious Connection

To write about the meaningful connections of one's life and not deal with the religious experience would seem to be indefensible, yet the very nature of the subject makes such an attempt seem insurmountable. Maybe it's because so many religious issues and beliefs such as prayer in public schools, opposition to abortion, homosexual rights, and funding for the arts when such expression is viewed as being indecent or obscene have been so controversial in the political arena. Maybe it's because my own religious connections have suffered frequent periods of disconnectedness, and this was true when Helen and I retired in the fall of 1984. Or maybe it has to do with the fact that, while I have grown more tolerant of other people's views about a wide range of issues through the years—some might say I've grown more liberal, even more permissive—many friends and acquaintances have clung to religious views that now may be labeled as "fundamentalist," a name many wear with pride.

I take some comfort from a book I read recent-

ly, *The Christian Agnostic*, by Leslie D. Weatherhead, an Englishman and a retired Methodist minister. Weatherhead wrote that he grudged the word
"fundamentalist" to those who are usually labeled
with it, and shared the word "agnostic" with those
who are smeared with it. But he concluded, "For
me, the area of 'fundamentals' grows smaller as I
grow older, and the area of agnosticism—in which
one says, 'I don't know'—grows larger. But this, I
think, is gain and, in a growing mind, inevitable."

Looking back, my earliest memory of attending
church was with my parents who infrequently
went to Bell Missionary Baptist Church in Haines
Township south of Salem near where they then
farmed. The minister may or may not have shared
the views of fundamentalists today, but he spoke
loudly and with authority, and it was a message of
hellfire and damnation. I can still remember his
harangue about the evils of wealth, and that morning he spoke of John D. Rockefeller, the robber
baron of history who was suffering from some
stomach malady at the time. I don't remember the
details, but the gist of the minister's message was
that God was punishing the Standard Oil tycoon
for both his wealth and the way in which he had
gained it.

In retrospect, church attendance apparently
was not a high priority for my parents, and as a boy
I don't recall that religion was often discussed in

our home. I do remember my mother dismissing this or that religious doctrine she didn't agree with, declaring that the Bible warned about "false prophets." But my mother was a skeptic about a lot of things. I remember her frequent dismissal of some compliment as being "blarney," meaning that the compliment was not sincere. That puzzled me at the time. I wondered why someone would say such things, particularly if my mother knew the speaker didn't mean it. My father was more trusting and believing about a lot of things. He enjoyed watching wrestling on television, for example, and resisted any effort by his son to discredit such antics as a legitimate sport. But my father had a low opinion of preachers in general.

Today the gospel is still being preached from Bell Missionary Baptist Church, now from a new building located across the road from the cemetery where my parents and older sister, Ruby, are buried. I hope and trust that more compassion for the sick, even those who may have prospered financially, is in evidence as the minister stands to speak each Sunday morning.

My own conversion to Christianity came as a teenager, and I presume it was not untypical of the experience of thousands of others in Christian evangelical churches throughout the rural Midwest. It came during an altar call following a fear-arousing appeal by the minister in a rural church south of Salem during a Sunday evening religious service. I was one of a group of four or five boys who went forward during the extended invitation. Despite my shyness, I felt compelled to join the others who had answered the minister's appeal. I remember some concern being expressed by church members about our action: What had triggered our decision? Why after all this time were we now coming forward? There also was some concern because most of us were not connected with church families. We were all baptized a couple of Sundays later in a farm pond across the road from the church. I can still feel the mud between my toes as we waded barefooted into the deeper water of the pond to await our turn to be immersed by the pastor as members of the congregation gathered at the water's edge and sang a hymn.

The church, Bethlehem Missionary Baptist, is still in the business of saving souls today, and from the size and condition of the sanctuary it must be prospering. During the mid-thirties when I attended, the church attracted several young people who found it a good place to meet other teenagers. I can still remember our Sunday School class, taught by the father of one of my classmates, which met in the choir loft, an elevated area to the left of the lectern from which the pastor preached every Sunday. A huge stove then sat in the middle of the wide center aisle, which warmed those nearby during cold weather but did little for those seated at the other end of the pews. After attending the services on Sunday morning, a group of young people often gathered at the home of one of the participants for a game of softball or some other form of "fellow-ship," as church elders labeled such activity. That evening, we sometimes returned to church for reli-gious services.

I can't remember much about any religious teaching from the Bethlehem experience, but I do remember that there was a lot of walking involved, especially for me since my parents then lived almost three miles from the church. Somehow it always seemed longer walking home after dark fol-lowing the evening service than it had earlier in the day when I had set off on foot in anticipation of the day's activities, which may have been the reason that I attended church infrequently.

Some of the relationships formed at Bethlehem Baptist, however, did influence my religious think-ing and helped to mold early views of what it meant to be a Christian. I remember the comfort that I received from assurances that once saved one was always saved despite any measure of "back-sliding," a concept I don't hear often anymore. But through the years I have noted a measure of growth as well as backsliding among the Bethlehem youth of the 1930s, and sometimes both are demonstrat-ed in the life of the same person. At one extreme was a lad I was to serve with for several years in the Army during World War II who died young of alcoholism. At the other extreme was a young woman, who I will call Jerrie, who spent most of her life as an outspoken apostle of her religious convictions, a sort of Jeremiah condemning the lifestyles of those who failed to measure up. In retrospect, I liked Jerrie better before she got religion. I would argue that I fell somewhere near the middle of such a religious continuum.

The religious connection experienced at Bethlehem became disconnected during the war years, was reconnected later at Salem First Baptist Church during the late 1940s, slowed during my years as a student at the University of Missouri in Columbia in the 1950s, spluttered now and then during my newspaper publishing years at Arcola, finally becoming disconnected once again while studying for a doctorate and teaching at Southern Illinois University at Carbondale.

The most intense period of religious activity through the years for me was during the post-war period, 1945-1950, at First Baptist in Salem, an active Southern Baptist church. I still have a photo in an album of a group of returning military veterans taken at a party sponsored by the church. It was held at the Masonic Temple across from the church after the war ended. There must have been forty honored guests who posed in their silly party hats, most of them young men, but a few women, too. I was not then a member of the church, but I had attended from time to time while working at Kohrig's Bakery before the war.

First Baptist had grown during the war years, largely because of the oil boom during the early 1940s which had brought numerous oil families to Salem from Oklahoma, Texas, and elsewhere in the Southwest, and many of them were Baptists. Soon afterward, Helen and I joined the church: me by letter from Bethlehem and Helen from Trinity Methodist Church in Salem. Every time the church doors opened, it seemed, we were there: Sunday School and morning worship and in the evening Training Union followed by evening worship. During the week, there were other activities: meetings of the Baptist men, the Women's Missionary Union, Bible study groups, and on Wednesday evening the Sunday School teachers meeting, followed by midweek worship services. Then there were frequent weddings and sometimes funerals. These were the years when most homes had no television and the church was a place for social as well as religious activity.

I became involved first as the adult department superintendent of the Sunday School and later was named as Sunday School superintendent with a staff and faculty of more than one hundred; Helen was also involved in various Sunday School positions. A sense of excitement and accomplishment was encouraged by the pastor, the Rev. James M. Baldwin, an excellent speaker with an engaging personality and an ardent believer in tithing. It wasn't long before the church outgrew its building on South Broadway and plans were underway for a new church on West Main Street. It was in the midst of this expansion that Helen and I decided to move from Salem so that I could attend the University of Missouri. The farewell following a Sunday morning service was an emotional parting for both of us. After all the goodbyes, I remember quizzing the pastor about what we might expect to encounter in our academic venture.

"Well, what are you looking for?" he asked.

We talked for a few minutes about our hopes and aspirations, mostly about positive aspects of the challenges we were facing.

"That's what you will find," he said. He was right, of course, but we never did find a church that came up to what we had experienced in Salem, and we were to be members of four Baptist churches during the next thirty years. That was partly because the First Baptist Church of Salem at that time was unique with a sense of mission that challenged us all. The other part of the problem was that we not only changed our address four times in the intervening years, but we changed also and continued to change with every passing year.

If change is inevitable under conditions that bring about a growing mind, as suggested by Leslie Weatherhead, it should not be surprising that my exposure to a multitude of teachers and the materials presented through their lectures and the assigned readings in my pursuit of three academic degrees would eventually produce change in many areas, including the modification of my religious beliefs and values. It's difficult to put one's finger on which teacher or what course of study may have been most influential in broadening my religious horizons, but a few stand out.

As an undergraduate at the University of Missouri, for example, I signed up for a course in comparative religion offered by the Missouri School of Religion located just off campus in Lowry Hall. I don't remember what attracted me to the course, but it seemed to be an interesting elective. I can still remember the professor who seemed to be forever surrounded by religious artifacts from various world religions he lectured about and who sometimes burned incense while we were taking examinations to enhance our religious experience. I remember also the general discomfort this exposure brought, particularly when I learned that Christianity didn't play the same role in the professor's scheme of things as it did in mine, and that Christianity represented only some fifteen percent of the world's religions.

This was followed by a course in comparative philosophy in which class members studied a different philosopher's work each week, which was enough to unsettle almost anyone's religious moorings. My response at the time was to sign up the following semester for a course in Old Testament history sponsored by the Baptist Foundation located on campus. The thought was that this would get my feet back on firmer ground, but the result was tentative at best.

It was exposure to American literature, a minor concentration during study for a doctorate at Southern Illinois University at Carbondale, that may have tested some of my more parochial religious precepts even more. I became fascinated, for example, with the transcendental writing of Ralph Waldo Emerson, a Unitarian minister, poet, and ethical thinker, and a pivotal figure in American literary history. I never fully understood his concept of the "Over-Soul" and the "Universal Mind," nor did I always grasp his transcendental philosophy with its assumption that "existence precedes essence," but much he wrote made good sense to me. I remember a passage in "The Divinity School Address" in which he describes a preacher he once had heard who sorely tempted him to say that he would "go to church no more." Emerson wrote the following:

"A snow-storm was falling around us. The

snow-storm was real, the preacher merely spectral, and the eye felt the sad contrast in looking at him, and then out of the window behind him into the beautiful meteor of the snow. He had lived in vain. He had no one word intimating that he had laughed or wept, was married or in love, had been commended, or cheated, or chagrined. If he had ever lived and acted, we were none the wiser for it. The capital secret of his profession, namely, to convert life into truth, he had not learned. Not one fact in all his experience had he yet imported into his doctrine."

I underlined that passage in the textbook more than twenty years ago. It's the best putdown of a minister, or of a teacher, I have ever read. It also is an interesting commentary on Emerson's philosophical assumption about existence preceding essence.

In a literature course examining American thought and writing during the colonial period, I was exposed to the sometimes harsh views of Puritan writers, many of them ministers, who demanded deep and constant thought about the nature of man and his relation to God, about man's duties to God and his neighbors and the high seriousness of life in this world. They included Increase and Cotton Mather, Jonathan Edwards, Roger Williams, and finally, Thomas Hooker, whose efforts produced Puritan writing at its best. The professor who taught the course, himself an ordained minister, didn't much like the Puritans, nor did I.

Another literature course focused on the writing of Nathaniel Hawthorne with its recurring images of guilt, isolation, emotional coldness, and death. And there was a seminar on the writings of Mark Twain that included his later writings and his dreary penchant for determinism as the humorist's usual lightheartedness turned to melancholy and darkness. This despite Twain's long friendship with the Rev. Joseph H. Twichell, a Congregational clergyman from Hartford, Connecticut, where Twain lived the last forty years of his life. During these dark years, Twain came to view God as being indifferent to man's fate and wrote that man had become the butt of nature's practical joke. How could this exuberant frontier humorist and the author of *Tom Sawyer* and *Huckleberry Finn* which have delighted young readers for generations come to such an end?

A more recent literature course, audited since my retirement, examining American fiction of the twentieth century, including such writers as Fitzgerald, Hemingway, Faulkner, Salinger, Bellow, Vonnegut, and other lesser writers, opened up yet other philosophical vistas for me. It wasn't just the unconventional lifestyles of several of the writers, which was amazing enough, it was also the themes they developed in their writings and the source of those themes. There was T. S. Eliot's *The Waste Land* with its image of suspended life—a sort of death-in-life—from which death proper would be an escape.

And existentialism, which dominated American fiction during the post-World War II years, was revisited by the instructor, who introduced the dualism and pessimism of Jean-Paul Satre, the principal exponent of existentialism in France, into our discussion and the philosophical notion of the "absurd" flowing from the writing of another Frenchman, Albert Camus, and Paul Tillich a German-born theologian and a Christian existentialist involved for a time in the religious colony at New Harmony, Indiana. I don't remember much of the philosophical tenets discussed in the class, but I still think of Satre's pessimistic view of life symbolized by a man standing on a cliff looking into space with only two choices: to live or to die by plunging into the abyss.

During this period when I was being exposed to all these "worldly" influences, there was a resurgence of conservative political thought bolstered by the rising voices of the religious right: the Rev. Jerry Falwell and his Moral Majority; the Rev. Pat Robertson and his 700 Club and his more recent efforts to take over local school boards; and the often strident anti-abortion voices of Operation Rescue members. It was during this time that lead-

ership of the Southern Baptist Convention was
being taken over by conservatives, and there followed a purging of Convention committees and
boards of those with more moderate views and
with dismissing faculty members at Southern Baptist seminaries who, in the pursuit of their research
and teaching, may have espoused views that conflicted with the doctrine of "inerrancy," the infalli-
bility of Biblical scripture. It was particularly offen-
sive to me when editors of Baptist newspapers
were sometimes censored or dismissed by church
leaders when their papers published stories that in
some way brought into question any such doctrine
of the church.

It was at this time that I was teaching university students taking press law that the First Amendment of the United States Constitution and its freedom of expression guarantees served to provide a
"marketplace of ideas," to use Justice Oliver Wendell Holmes' term, from which truth would
emerge. And as a teacher at a public university, that
same First Amendment provided me with a measure of academic freedom to follow my scholarly
pursuits for truth wherever they might lead me.
The Baptist seminaries, of course, were private
schools and denominational newspapers were pri-
vately owned and were, therefore, not subject to
First Amendment safeguards. But such undemo-
cratic and authoritarian actions still disturbed me,

and for this as well as other reasons my attendance at church became less and less frequent.

After our retirement in the fall of 1984, Helen and I avowed to one another that we were going to get involved once again in a church where we could renew our religious connections. Soon afterward, we returned one Sunday morning to the Walnut Street Baptist Church in Carbondale where our membership still resided. The visit did little to rekindle our religious faith, however, and for the next three years we drifted from one church to another, attending irregularly and finding little joy in the effort. We visited University Baptist near the SIUC campus, First Baptist downtown, and finally we showed up one Sunday morning at First United Methodist Church. Helen had been a Methodist in Salem when we were married. We didn't plan to remain in Carbondale, we told ourselves; indeed, we were looking elsewhere for a retirement home. While we continued attending First Methodist, we viewed ourselves as visitors still in search of a home.

That search took us to the Southwest a couple of times: San Antonio, Tucson, San Diego, and finally to Phoenix where Sun City attracted our attention. The other magnet in the Phoenix area, of course, was my favorite niece, Beverly, in nearby Scottsdale. Helen and I had both been attracted to the beauty of the Southwest and the abundant housing, including Beverly's new home in Paradise Valley. We also enjoyed attending Sunday morning worship services with Beverly and her family in the beautiful Valley Presbyterian Church where the order of worship and the responsive readings seemed amazingly similar to that of the Methodists.

As I listened to the Presbyterian minister that morning, my thoughts wandered to the stern moral code of Calvinism that I had been introduced to in that SIUC course in American thought and writing during the colonial period. I listened also for some hint of the doctrine of predestination which one might expect from a follower of John Calvin, but I detected none. I was reminded that I had encountered predestination first in a Puritan context, which probably befits the doctrine better than in Scottsdale where evidence of affluence was all around us.

During the spring quarter of 1987, I taught at the University of Tennessee in Knoxville and we continued exploring different churches on Sunday mornings, both Baptist and Methodist, and we learned that Knoxville had a host of churches. Central Baptist near our little apartment had a membership of more than 3,000 and boasted seven seminary-trained ministers who headed up the various departments of the church. It was a joy to sit in the huge, beautifully decorated sanctuary, but the religious doctrine communicated from the pulpit, despite the skill and training of the learned staff, was less than inspiring. We also attended the stately Church Street United Methodist Church downtown overlooking the Tennessee River and were impressed with the dignity and solemnity of the more formal order of worship. As a visiting professor at the university, we were always made welcome, but we remained just that—visitors.

After returning to Carbondale in June, Helen and I began to reevaluate our plans for retirement in earnest. Florida, the Gulf Coast, and more recently, Arizona, all had their appeal, and for the first time in our lives we felt free to move anywhere we wanted to go. My mother had died in February and, as the eldest son and with Helen's assistance, I had completed work to close her estate. We had no relatives in Carbondale, and we were in agreement that there was no compelling reason to remain; indeed, most retired faculty from the university seemed to have moved elsewhere.

But faced squarely with such a decision, Carbondale, for some reason, started to compare more favorably with the adult communities in the Southland we had been looking at for so many months, and our home at 305 Canterbury Drive started to outshine the condos we had dreamed of owning— at least with a little remodeling it would compare well. A former faculty colleague, writing recently for the *Southern Illinoisan*, perhaps expressed it best. He wrote that his impatience to return to Southern Illinois after living in the big city had nothing to do with nostalgia, which properly belongs to those born and bred in the area, nor was it like Stevenson's poem about the hunter home from the hill. It was more like the slow realization that an acquaintance you once thought dull and pedestrian turned out to be witty, charming, gifted and intelligent and who you now consider to be a warm friend. I can identify with that. At about this time, First United Methodist Church also seemed to take on new life and seemed more appealing and desirable.

One of the attractions to the denomination for me was that Methodists do not agree on all aspects of religious doctrine. In a class for new members, the Rev. Don Carlton, pastor of First Methodist, set out four main guidelines to help class members understand the basis for their faith: the Scripture, religious tradition, individual experience, and the power of reason. Or as stated in the Methodist Book of Discipline, preaching and teaching should be "grounded in Scripture, informed by Christian tradition, enlivened in experience, and tested by reason." The acknowledgment that tradition plays a role in the formation of Methodist doctrine reminds me of Tevye's repeated explanation of doctrinal complexities in the musical *Fiddler on the Roof.* Such guidelines are viewed as interdependent and allow for variety in the theology of individual Methodists.

We also learned that Methodists share a common heritage with other Christians: a conviction that God has mercy and love for all people, belief in a triune God (Father, Son, and Holy Spirit) although John Wesley, the founder of Methodism, had problems with the concept of the Trinity; faith in the mystery of salvation through Jesus Christ; and celebration of the sacraments: baptism and the Lord's Supper. The class also dealt with the structure of the Methodist Church, which is organized for ministry at several levels, maintaining "connectional" links with one another. Though we were told this structure is what distinguishes Methodism from other denominations, and though the various governing bodies made up of both clergy and laity may be democratic, it is also complex and, for me, difficult to comprehend. Helen and I later served for three years on the administrative board of the church and I acted as publicity chairman for two years, but some things the Methodists do are still a mystery to me.

Exposure to the goings on in a rather unorthodox Sunday School class may have done more to stimulate religious thought these past few years, however, than anything heard from the pulpit. The class has viewed and discussed a series of video tapes entitled "Questions of Faith" in which religious leaders, teachers, and writers respond to scores of questions and with a diversity of answers. In one of the video series, for example, six questions were posed: What's the use of the Bible? Who's got the truth? How do we right the wrong? What gives you faith? What happens after death? Who is Jesus? These and additional subquestions are put to a panel of ministers, theologians, writers, and others with a variety of backgrounds who respond on the video, often in unexpected ways.

Excerpts from the answers to the question, "What's the use of the Bible?" may give some idea of the diversity of views held by such a panel: Rabbi Harold Kushner says he takes the Bible very seriously as the record of God's revelation. Jewish scholars have read the Torah not as a novel to see how it ends, Kushner says, but as a love letter. Rosemary Ruether, a Catholic theologian, points out that Jews don't accept the New Testament and Christians don't accept much of the Old Testament. Another Catholic theologian, Elisabeth Schussler-Fiorenza, believes the authority of the Bible is given in the people struggling to live the Christian vision. Will Campbell, a Baptist minister, thinks no one believes the Bible literally. John Spong, an Episcopal bishop, says the Bible has been ruined for most religious people by the kind of superstition that has been placed on it. Walter

Wink, a Methodist theologian, thinks people have been bullied by clergy into thinking they're not capable of interpreting scripture. And from such diversity of ideas truth should emerge?

Books of interest to class members are also read and discussed: Leslie Weatherhead's *The Christian Agnostic*, quoted from at the beginning of this chapter; M. Scott Peck's *The Road Less Traveled* and its 1993 update, *Further Along the Road Less Traveled*, both of which expound what this practicing psychiatrist calls a new psychology of love, traditional values and spiritual growth; and Rabbi Harold Kushner's *When Bad Things Happen to Good People* and *Who Needs God*. These discussions are generally led by a retired professor from SIUC and a long-time teacher of a course in educational psychology who usually poses far more questions than he answers.

The class also frequently hears from outside speakers: missionaries, a Muslim scholar, the director of a hospice organization, or the church pastor with a series on religious history. I find the sessions stimulating as diverse views are expressed by those with far more knowledge than either Helen or I have on the topic under discussion. But it is also discomforting at times, and unsettling, to find beliefs one once accepted as fundamental brought into serious question.

This stimulation of religious thought has

prompted a further quest for knowledge, which I have assumed is a healthy approach to living even though the challenges one finds may tend to further diminish the area of religious fundamentals one once held. If the national media are any barometer, there has been a growing interest in religious history and exploring religious practices.

A recent cover story in *U.S. News & World Report* entitled "Spiritual America" found that this nation "under God" is deeply conflicted over the role of religion in society. That same week, *Time* magazine carried a two-page story attempting to answer the question, "Why was Christ crucified?" and *Newsweek's* cover story in a pre-Easter issue discussed "The Death of Jesus" and "New Insights to the Gospels at the Core of Christianity." Recent news stories also report the findings of scholars making up the radical Jesus Seminar who have been examining the Gospels and voting on the authenticity of the sayings attributed to Jesus. One startling claim is that Jesus probably never uttered the Lord's Prayer as it is written in the Bible, although he may have used phrases in the prayer at various times during his ministry.

But far more challenging to traditional religious doctrine for me has been the outpouring of provocative books in recent years, some such as *The Dead Sea Scrolls Deception* by Michael Baigent and Richard Leigh and *The Lost Gospel:*

The Book of Q by Burton L. Mack based on new archaeological discoveries. Other recent books are based on research of revisionist biblical historians.

An incredible example of the broad scope of such books is Karen Armstrong's *A History of God: The 4,000-Year Quest of Judaism, Christianity and Islam,* published in 1993. The author argues that God cannot be expected to be experienced as objective fact that could be discovered by the ordinary process of rational thought. In an important sense, she writes, God is the product of the creative imagination, like poetry and music that one finds so inspiring. And the idea of God formed by one generation, by one set of human beings could be meaningless in another, a view fundamentalists would certainly deny.

Then there are recent books about Jesus: *The Historical Jesus,* subtitled "The Life of a Mediterranean Jewish Peasant," and *Jesus: A Revolutionary Biography,* both by John Dominic Crossan, a professor of biblical studies at DePaul University in Chicago, who views Jesus as a social revolutionary and argues that the resurrection is a myth; and *Jesus: A Life* by A. N. Wilson, a liberal critic of the idea that Jesus was a divine messiah and savior; and *The Unauthorized Version* by Robin Lane Fox, which questions whether the Bible is a reliable witness to the historical events it records.

These books, some more polemic than others,

may seem strangely out of place on the same book-shelf in my study with the writings of John Wesley, Leslie Weatherhead, Harold Kushner, Billy Graham, and other more traditional Bible scholars. However critical and challenging, I find it difficult to ignore their contribution to biblical scholarship.

Even more provocative is that champion of free thinking in the area of religion and theology, *Free Inquiry*, published quarterly by the Council for Democratic and Secular Humanism. I subscribed to the magazine for a couple of years to learn more about secular humanism while, at the same time, Helen and I were helping to finance a young man involved with a more traditional religious group who said they were trying to stamp out secular humanism in Southern Illinois high schools. I just wanted to learn more about the evil doctrine and why it should be eradicated. As it turns out, *Free Inquiry* is more focused on free thought and free will than in propagating any religious heresy. Such freedom, even as guaranteed by the free exercise clause of the First Amendment, of course, includes an individual's right to reject religion. And the more radical poses the magazine takes seems more a counterpoise to the extremism of the religious right than any threat to the free exercise of one's religion.

Noah Webster defines humanism as a system of thought based on the nature, dignity, interests, and ideals of man, specifically, a modern, nontheistic, rationalist movement that holds that man is capable of self-fulfillment, ethical conduct, etc., without recourse to supernaturalism. It seems reasonable that a person with such views might well hold that those who block abortion clinic entrances, who attempt to censor textbooks and curricula, and who attempt to use the media to infuse a fear of free thought, to be "armies of zealots," as did a recent mailing from the editor of *Free Inquiry*. The First Amendment establishment clause, of course, as interpreted by the U.S. Supreme Court, arguably holds that neither secular humanism nor more traditional religious doctrine should be taught in public school classrooms.

Through the years, as I have grown more skeptical about the religious teachings of my youth, those who were the source of those teachings, at least as a denomination, have grown more conservative and authoritarian. But even as a Christian agnostic, to use Weatherhead's label, I believe in God as a universal spirit as apparently some ninety-three percent of all Americans do—if one can believe polling results—but for me God is less personal than he once was and apparently still is to a majority of Americans, including those who count themselves as fundamentalists. The idea of some divine intervention or special providence protecting one's livelihood may be comforting, but the apparent randomness of the victims of crime and violence brings such an idea into question. The tornado that struck the Goshen United Methodist Church in Alabama on a recent Palm Sunday, killing twenty and injuring ninety during the morning worship services, makes one wonder where even a Christian can find a safe haven.

I also have come to reject the view that the Bible is literally true in all its parts, as do the majority of Americans, and acknowledge that some of the Bible may be based upon myth which, nevertheless, may still contain truths—a view of Scott Peck and Joseph Campbell. The doctrine of "inerrancy" espoused by those who proudly wear the fundamentalist label, however, appears intellectually unacceptable if that term is itself to be taken literally. I believe in the historical Jesus and find inspiration in His example and His teachings, as do most Christians, and though my heart yearns to accept the resurrection story, when reason takes precedence I am troubled by the writing of biblical historians, many of whom find the resurrection to be based on myth, not historical fact.

I have found that it's easier, however, to accept the message, "He is not here, He is risen," a statement that graced our church bulletin on Easter Sunday, when the heart gets more involved and the choir, accompanied by the hand bells and brass, renders its "Anthem for Resurrection" and the pastor, in a special effort before the enlarged religious holiday crowd, has completed his uplifting sermon,

When the congregation stands to sing "Christ Is Alive" as a sending forth hymn, and Helen places her hand over mine on the back of the pew in front of us during the benediction, it's easier then to have faith that everything is going to be all right. Suddenly one of the most memorable Bible verses learned in my youth comes to mind: "Faith is the substance of things hoped for, the evidence of things not seen." (Hebrews 11.1) The intellect may say there should be more than hope, but the heart at such times is willing to nurture faith in the promise.

The Senior Connection

The senior connection has to do with growing old, a prospect that most face with
some reluctance though the process
appears inevitable. A recent *Parade* magazine sur-
vey examining attitudes toward aging and the
elderly found that two-thirds of the respondents
said old age begins at seventy or older. Among
these, twenty-eight percent didn't consider someone old until eighty and beyond. In general, the
older the respondents, the older the age that they
defined as "old." Among respondents over sixty-
five, for example, only eight percent thought of
people under sixty-five as being old, but thirty percent of those under twenty-five said "old" was anywhere from forty to sixty-four.

For Helen and me, the senior connection came
about incrementally. Helen joined the American
Association of Retired Persons (AARP) years ago,
long before she retired from work, when eligibility
for membership began at fifty-five. The AARP has
since lowered the entry age to fifty. It wasn't that
she was anxious to become connected with the

senior crowd. Membership in AARP had become a good way to establish eligibility for senior discounts, particularly when making motel and hotel reservations. I have never felt the need to join the AARP since we generally travel and sleep together. My first senior connection, I suppose, was at age sixty when a modest pension first arrived from the U.S. Department of Defense based upon twenty years of active and reserve military service. I remember the twinge of sadness that acceptance of the pension brought, but economic considerations prevailed and I kept the check.

It was retirement, however, that accelerated our move toward senior status. It was preceded, of course, with much planning and agonizing. Was it the right time to retire? After retirement, we no longer needed to remain in Carbondale, but where would we move? Will we have enough money to be comfortable in retirement? As we grow older, will we be able to take care of our home? Will our health insurance be sufficient? Should we make contingency plans for retirement living? For assisted care living? For long-term health care? When we finally decided to retire in the fall of 1984, we hadn't satisfactorily answered these questions.

Ten years later some of those concerns still aren't settled. We are still in Carbondale, and we still care for our home with no contingency plans for assisted living, which will one day come, with-

out doubt. Our retirement income still meets our
needs though our interest income has been
reduced more than fifty percent since retirement
because of falling interest rates. But in the process
of retirement, we have conclusively joined the
ranks of senior citizens. I suppose that recognition
came for me when I reached my seventieth birthday, my hairline receding and my waist expanding
under my Sansabelt slacks, that denial of senior
status seemed to be pointless. But by then Helen
and I had become involved in so many activities
that the process of growing old had lost some of
the anxiety and dread it had once brought.

The freedom to travel is one of the immediate
joys of being retired. To be sure there were vaca-
tions and some opportunity to travel in connection
with one's employment, but the deadlines and other time restraints limit the joy of such travel. In
retirement, the open road often beckons and the
duration of the journey is limited only by one's
energy and the resources flowing from the credit
cards in one's pocket. Surprisingly, we haven't
been on an airplane since our retirement, but we
have kept the interstate highways busy as we have
piled up almost 200,000 frequent driver miles during the past ten years. Our more extensive trips
have been the annual treks to the Southland each
February where we visit with friends and motel
hop for two or three weeks to avoid the sometimes

frigid midwinter temperatures of Illinois.

Most of these auto trips have been to Florida where Orlando, Fort Myers, and Naples get the most attention, but a couple of February trips to Arizona have afforded a change of pace with the opportunity to visit with friends and relatives in the Southwest. Motel hopping, of course, isn't the best way to enjoy Florida or Arizona during the "snowbird" season, but without advance planning and preregistration one is often forced to move from place to place. We have promised ourselves that if we continue to spend February in the South we will make plans early enough to rent a condo or apartment and stay put for a more restful visit.

But a good part of the joy of travel for us has been the adventure of exploring new places, and looking back we have done our share of visiting attractions of interest to most tourists. We have walked the beaches of Hilton Head and Myrtle Beach, South Carolina; Daytona Beach, Florida; Gulf Shores, Alabama; and Gulfport and Biloxi, Mississippi. We have frequented the French Quarter of New Orleans; Fort Sumter and the historic district of Charleston, South Carolina; and Savannah, Georgia. We have enjoyed the arts and crafts of the Museum of Appalachia in Tennessee; at Berea, Kentucky; and in Eureka Springs, Arkansas.

East Tennessee has held a fascination for both Helen and me since I taught at the University of

Tennessee at Knoxville as a visiting professor in 1987, and we have returned frequently to enjoy the Dogwood Festival in Knoxville in April and to mix with the thousands of tourists who return to Pigeon Forge, Dollywood, and Gatlinburg every year to play, shop the scores of discount stores, and romp in the Great Smoky Mountains. And we are attracted to country music events at Nashville, Tennessee, and Branson, Missouri, where seniors flock during all seasons of the year. On one of our most memorable visits to Nashville, we joined a Prime Timers tour from our church for a two-night stay at the Opryland Hotel, where the buildings and grounds were decorated with thousands of lights, to participate in "A Country Christmas." We have also visited New Orleans frequently, a place that attracts many seniors for repeat visits. During the spring or fall, a stop off to tour the antebellum homes in Natchez, Mississippi, adds to the enjoyment of the trip South.

A more structured event involving travel for me has been attending the annual convention of journalism educators, the Association for Education in Journalism and Mass Communication (AEJMC), and the opportunity to visit with former journalism colleagues and students. Helen and I have attended six such conventions of the AEJMC, more than I attended when I taught: Gainesville, Florida; Memphis, Tennessee; Montreal, Canada;

Kansas City, Missouri; Minneapolis, Minnesota; and Atlanta, Georgia. Military reunions have afforded another opportunity for travel, particularly when they were held in such places as Kansas City, Tucson, Boston, Scottsdale, and Nashville. Sometimes travel affords the opportunity to visit with friends and relatives in interesting places as did our trips to Oxford, Ohio; Raleigh, North Carolina; Fairhope, Alabama; Oxford, Mississippi; and San Diego, California.

After such journeys, of course, it's always a pleasure to return home, at least for a while. One of our neighbors seems to have the best arrangement for travel in retirement. Julius and Helen hook their Airstream trailer to their Suburban and disappear for weeks, sometimes months. They returned recently after spending the winter in an Airstream facility near Dade City, Florida.

One of the real pleasures of retirement for me has been the opportunity for leisure reading, something I struggled to make time for while I faced newspaper deadlines and during the years that I taught journalism. Ironically I now have no newspaper column or students with whom to share my newly acquired insights from this reading. After retirement, I audited courses at the university for several semesters, including those on the history of the antebellum South and American fiction of the twentieth century. There was really no purpose in taking the courses other than the pleasure of reading and discussing them with others.

That same impulse toward books and reading may explain why I find myself browsing in bookstores in every mall Helen and I visit and in being tempted to rejoin the Book-of-the-Month Club every time I get a mailing offering four books for a dollar each. But I don't really need to acquire additional books; hundreds of them already fill bookcases that line my study walls and others scattered throughout our home. I've explored many of those books since retirement, including Dumas Malone's six-volume biography of Thomas Jefferson, the last of which, *The Sage of Monticello*, deals with Jefferson's active retirement, including his efforts in establishing the University of Virginia. Shelby Foote's massive three-volume narrative history of the Civil War sets on a bookshelf above my desk; I'm going to get around to reading this account of the war one of these days.

Recently, I've been more attracted to books that are more entertaining and less scholarly. I was introduced to Robert Fulghum's little books in 1989 with the publication of *All I Really Need to Know I Learned in Kindergarten*. Three more little Fulghum books with strange titles have followed, all equally enjoyable. I also discovered Garrison Keillor in *Lake Wobegon Days*, and there have followed other books filled with charming little stories and satirical essays from this master storyteller. More recently, I was compelled to learn why Robert Waller's little book, *The Bridges of Madison County*, was making this former college dean a rich man. His *Slow Waltz in Cedar Bend* has followed, which has a similar plot but the scene shifts from an Iowa farmstead to a college campus, and the republication of some of Waller's earlier essays, which first appeared in Iowa newspapers entitled *Old Songs in a New Cafe*. Many critics don't like Waller, but millions of readers apparently do.

Many of the 40,000 books published each year are soon forgotten, but I was particularly attracted to a couple of Pulitzer Prize-winning books, *Lonesome Dove* by Larry McMurtry, and William Kennedy's *Ironweed*, which probably has more literary merit. The novel *Hawaii* started a long relationship with James Michener, but his voluminous narratives have outstripped my energy to keep up with his constant scribbling. Indeed, my zest for reading has waned in recent years, which is regrettable. So much on television, to which one can easily become addicted, is a waste of time.

I've never been much of a joiner when it comes to civic, social, or fraternal organizations. I have never considered time spent at such activities as being particularly important or worthwhile. Yes, I did become an Optimist and later a Lion as a newspaper editor and publisher, but my heart really wasn't in either organization. My participation was more of a public relations effort than any real dedication to the high ideals of being an Optimist or a Lion. But in retirement and as a senior citizen, my perspective has undergone a metamorphosis. Organizations, from those associated with the First United Methodist Church to the luncheon group of the local AARP, seem to form the structure of many of the daily relationships of the seniors with whom Helen and I are involved.

About the time we retired, First Methodist organized a monthly luncheon for seniors who meet in the church's Fellowship Hall for a catered meal and a program of interest to seniors. These Prime Timers, as they call themselves, are led by a lay staff member who also plans frequent trips to points of interest: St. Louis to take in a musical at the Muny Opera; a foliage tour through Southern Illinois in October; a three-day trip to Branson, Missouri, to attend a country music show or two and a visit to Silver Dollar City; or a bus tour to the Amish Country in Central Illinois. And more recently, a monthly schedule of breakfast or dinner outings for many of these same seniors, now called the Prime Time Players, who try out a variety of eating establishments in the area with nothing more on the agenda than eating and visiting.

The military and various organizations associated with the military are a source of social activity for many local seniors as well as younger military retirees. The Little Egypt Chapter of The Retired Officers Association (TROA), to which I belong, holds a Saturday evening dinner meeting each month at various Southern Illinois locations with Army, Marine, Navy, and Air Force retired officers mixing it up with tales of military exploits and of service in strange places around the world. Members of TROA recently took a Saturday afternoon for a trip on Merv Griffin's Riverboat Casino based in Metropolis to try their luck at the slot machines.

Then there are the Mustangers, members of the National Order of Battlefield Commissions (NOBC), who hold regional meetings, which few people attend, and national conventions in Las Vegas or some other tourist attraction, which many do attend to kick up their heels once a year. I was even persuaded in retirement to join the Veterans of Foreign Wars, but after two years and failure to attend a single meeting, I became a dropout.

Academic organizations still play a part in the life of seniors such as me, despite retirement. A local chapter of the State Universities Annuitants Association (SUAA) holds semiannual meetings to update its members on issues affecting retirement pay and other interests. The Emeritus Association of Southern Illinois University recruits members to work in three Red Cross blood drives each year and seeks volunteers for other campus tasks.

Membership in the President's Council, extended to those who establish scholarships or otherwise provide minimal endowments to the University Foundation, gets one invited to a couple of social functions each year on campus.

Then there is the Faculty Club for retired university faculty that holds a Sunday evening potluck on campus once a month to enjoy a program focused on some faculty interest. But the primary attraction appears to be the food, the main course of so many of these organizational activities. Helen belongs to the local chapter of the National Association of Retired Federal Employees (NARFE), which meets once a month for lunch at the Ponderosa West where the Grand Buffet virtually guarantees that you will eat too much. And even outside such organizational settings, an outing with just a couple of friends will more than likely end up being an occasion for dining out.

All this eating and the slowing of one's metabolism forces many seniors to undertake activities intended to safeguard physical fitness. One such activity that Helen and I have engaged in for several years is early morning walking at University Mall with scores of other seniors before the shops open. One lap around the inside of the mall is three-quarters of a mile if one explores each of the corridors leading to the various anchor stores. It's a rather pleasant stroll. The mall management supplies background music, and walkers generally greet one another on the first lap around. Often couples join one another to walk together.

Helen and I once walked together for three laps three or four mornings each week, but arthritic knees have slowed my pace and shortened my range so I now walk alone. As I hobble along, I'm reminded of Scott Peck's opening sentence in *The Road Less Traveled*: "Life is difficult." Every Wednesday from nine to ten, Cinnamon Sam's serves free coffee and miniature muffins to seniors. Other mornings seniors may end up at McDonald's across the highway from the mall. McDonald's seems to know how to treat both seniors and the younger fry. Children are attracted by Happy Meals and Ronald McDonald the clown; seniors are wooed by twenty-five cent drinks.

Life would be far less difficult than it often is for seniors, however, if a few laps around the mall several times a week would keep one's aging body shipshape. For the past two or three years Helen and I have probably spent more time at the Carbondale Clinic or in the waiting room of some medical specialist than we have walking the mall. There have also been infrequent out-patient visits to Carbondale Memorial Hospital and even a trip to the Mayo Clinic when health problems became too complicated. In the process, we have learned to become more involved in our own health care and have become more knowledgeable about medical procedures and pharmaceutical drugs.

We have accumulated a shelf of medical books: *Mayo Clinic Family Health Book*, *Physician's Desk Reference*, *People's Pharmacy for Older Adults*, *Worst Pill, Best Pills, Before You Call the Doctor (Safe Effective Self-Care for Over 300 Common Medical Problems)*, and other books dealing with high blood pressure, arthritis, symptoms, treatments, and home remedies.

I'm reminded that Dr. Scott Peck, who I've referred to frequently in these pages, recounts in *Further Along the Road Less Traveled* that about a decade after leaving medical school he discovered that doctors know very little about medicine. He discovered this, he said, when he stopped asking, "What do we know?" and began asking, "What don't we know?" Too often doctors, if they are honest, he writes, must answer, "We don't know." And Dr. Peck even suggests, perhaps tongue-in-cheek, that patients caught on some time ago that doctors don't know much.

But as seniors, Helen and I have learned to better appreciate the challenges that face physicians such as my favorite niece, Beverly, in the daily practice of medicine. In that learning process, even medical specialists, once difficult to identify with their area of expertise, have become more familiar.

At Mayo Clinic several years ago, Helen's primary doctor was an English woman who could talk faster than many seniors could think. She held forth in an office high up in the main Clinic building on a floor where more than fifty cardiologists saw patients. For four days we explored the pedestrian subways that linked our hotel to the various buildings housing laboratories and treatment facilities, including two hospitals operated by the Clinic, to consult with more specialists than we knew even existed. Concerns about cardiovascular fitness (hypertension, high cholesterol and dietary fats) had brought about Helen's referral to Mayo. There followed dozens of tests, including a radionuclide scan, which we learned was one of several types of angiograms, but no coronary angioplasty was warranted. It turned out to be a satisfying visit; the prognosis was generally good.

More recently, Helen and I became even more acutely aware of the serious nature of cardiovascular problems in our effort to support Amos and Betty as he underwent a series of operations at a St. Louis hospital. First it was discovered that Amos had a ninety percent blockage of the carotid artery on one side of his neck, and the plaque was promptly removed in a rather simple but dangerous endarterectomy surgical procedure. A few weeks later, after he had recovered from that bout, he underwent a lengthy surgery to repair a large, life-threatening abdominal aortic aneurysm. In the process, or "on the way out," as the surgeon put it, his gall bladder was removed. But in a follow-up angiogram, the catheterization caused a blood clot that kept him hospitalized for several days longer. While we were present in only a supporting role, seeing a brother going under the knife time after time is a traumatic experience, and we learned a lot about the aggressiveness of some surgeons.

Less traumatic but frustrating nevertheless has been the day-to-day treatment of glaucoma, which Helen and I have both been engaged in for several years in an effort to control the high pressure in our eyes that can damage the optic nerve and even lead to blindness. My mother went blind in her later years because of glaucoma, which I'm told makes my elevated pressure even more threatening. Helen and I see the same ophthalmologist, a Nigerian and one of six such specialists operating out of the Marion Eye Center, which has a branch office in Carbondale. We administer eye drops to one another twice daily, and hope the drugs—we each have a different ophthalmic prescription—continue to be effective. Helen has had two laser procedures in each eye in an effort to further lower the pressure; I've had a tear in the retina of the left eye repaired by laser.

We are both developing cataracts, which we're told will be the experience of most seniors if we continue to live longer and longer. We sat with our friend Millie recently in the waiting room of the Marion Surgical Center as her husband, Bob, had cataracts removed, first in one eye and a few weeks later in the other eye. A videotape played on the television monitor and, each time it was completed, an aide who kept crossing the reception room leading patients to their cars, punched the button to start it over again. After nearly three hours, I felt that I could repeat verbatim the ophthalmologist's message on caring for the eye following surgery.

I also marvelled at the number of patients, most of them seniors, who kept emerging from the backrooms of the Center with patches over an eye, and wondered how much the morning's work of this one ophthalmologist, who advertised he had done some 30,000 such procedures, was costing Medicare that day—or whatever other health insurance might be involved.

My primary physical affliction is more commonplace. My doctor, who is a rheumatologist as well as an internist, calls it degenerative or osteoarthritis most of the time, but in the shoulder it becomes bursitis or tendinitis and may call for a shot of cortisone, and in the fingers its tenosynovitis or "trigger finger," at least in my case. A couple of times, a plastic surgeon, who also specializes in repairing hands, has surgically split the sheath that protects the tendon to the afflicted finger, allowing it to function properly once again. Three other fingers have since become candidates for "untriggering." But it is the knees that give me the most trouble. I have a shelf of anti-inflammatory drugs that have been prescribed from time to time, but after a few days my stomach refuses to cooperate.

An orthopedic surgeon started me on a program of therapy several years ago, which was on-again, off-again for many months but has turned into a daily regimen. Therapy has been an effort to avoid arthroscopic surgery, which in my case would be to clean up calcium deposits under the knee caps that under conditions of too much stress damage the cartilage in the knee joints. Before therapy, I could hardly walk across the living room because of the pain. I can now walk at a fairly normal gate on level ground, but climbing stairs, particularly when carrying baggage or other heavy objects, soon messes things up. We have learned to make reservations for lower-level rooms to avoid stairs or to choose motels with at least three levels, which usually guarantees there will be an elevator.

My surgeon says that if worst comes to worst the knee joint can be replaced with a prosthesis. Recently a friend of Helen's set out to have arthroscopic surgery on both knees but, after a prolonged period of recovery and a round of painful therapy following surgery to the first knee, she proclaimed that the second knee no longer bothered her. I'm reminded that my mother always related her arthritis to the weather and would let us all know when conditions worsened and her arthritis "flared up," as she put it. I used to think that this was a quaint way of viewing and explaining such an ailment, but recently I picked up a magazine in the Carbondale Clinic waiting room edited for those suffering from arthritis and found a column discussing the writer's "flares" with arthritis. Technology may have changed through the years, but the "flares" apparently have remained the same.

We have also recently gained first-hand knowledge about other medical specialists. There is the guy who administers anesthetics and monitors the anesthesia process before, during, and after surgery—the anesthesiologist. My first "trigger finger" surgery didn't go well when the tourniquet used in the block of my left arm apparently was removed too quickly. I ended up in recovery for more than an hour watching two bottles of IV drip into my good arm while Helen waited patiently downstairs. The second surgery went better and the anesthesiologist sent me on my way in record time. And Helen has a dermatologist who specializes in the diagnosis and treatment of skin diseases. A retired military associate who was a dermatologist in the Navy before practicing in Carbondale after his military retirement, used to say that one advantage of being a dermatologist was that patients generally never get well, but they seldom die.

But the medical specialist with the most difficult title must be the otorhinolaryngologist, sometimes designated as ENT, who specializes in disorders of the ears, nose, throat and related regions. I see one from time to time for a throat examination, especially when difficulty in swallowing reoccurs, as it often does. He generally does a procedure called a laryngoscopy in which a fiberoptic endoscope is inserted into my nose and carefully threaded down my throat into my larynx allowing the doctor to diagnose or rule out a health problem. I have feared that many years of pipe smoking as a young man may have brought on my throat problem. The diagnosis thus far: "There is no growth or obstruction; you will just have to live with your swallowing problem." Which is better than being referred to an oncologist, a medical specialist I hope to never visit.

Helen and I, like most seniors, have been involved also in educating ourselves about the need for health care in future years as we grow older and making provisions about who is to make health care decisions for us. There have been seminars about the function of living wills and the purpose of power of attorney for health care as recently authorized by the Illinois General Assembly. We both signed a power of attorney for health care in 1990 shortly after the new Illinois statute became effective and which, among other provisions, sets out the level of life-sustaining treatment we wish that agent to take. It states these terms:

"I do not want my life to be prolonged nor do I want life-sustaining treatment to be provided or continued if my agent believes the burdens of the treatment outweigh the expected benefits. I want my agent to consider the relief of suffering, the expense involved and the quality as well as the possible extension of my life in making decisions concerning life-sustaining treatment."

That's quite a burden to place on anyone, but it seems the logical choice among the three offered under the law. The same day, we each signed a legal document setting up a power of attorney for property. A few months later, we signed a living trust — in legal jargon, a "Joint Declaration of Trust"— upon the advice of attorney. This, in turn, required a new "pour over" will to supplement the effect of the trust. We found this to be weighty stuff that tends to make one feel more senior than usual. In fact, such legal dealings, though probably necessary for seniors, can be downright depressing.

A few of our senior friends have gone even a step further in planning for the future—or for their final exit. They have purchased their tombstones and had them placed on cemetery lots with their names freshly engraved for all to see. I brought this subject up one day recently with Helen as I was scanning the obituary columns of the *Salem Times-Commoner*, which had just arrived in the mail. We had returned a few days earlier from our annual pre-Memorial Day visit to area cemeteries to decorate the graves of our parents and other relatives and to place a red rose beside the white cross bearing the name of Helen's father located in a sea of crosses in the corner of the Salem cemetery to honor the dead of past wars.

But generally we make it a habit to stay away from cemeteries. As to the purchase of a tombstone, even if we did it now we likely couldn't agree on where to place it. We have moved around too much through the years, and even if one wanted to go home again, which home should it be? But the real reason that we haven't purchased a tombstone is that such an action would seem to be encouraging the inevitable, and we really don't plan to need such a marker for a while yet.

Epilogue

I received a brochure through the mail recently advertising a new magazine, *Good Old Days*, which was billed as "The magazine that remembers the best." That caught my eye, the part about remembering the best, which is what I've been attempting in these little essays focusing on the meaningful connections of my life. The magazine's editor pointed out that as a boy arrowheads were pretty common and that his father had quite a collection of them. He surmised that the stories in his new magazine were a lot like arrowheads.

"Each one is a commonplace treasure, wrought from the American soul. Each one is a gem, tempered by time, the hearty experience of people who built this country. As I look back over the years I think of the arrowheads of my youth, and of all the other warm memories stretching from those days up to the present," he wrote. I like that phrase, "the arrowheads of my youth."

I haven't subscribed to *Good Old Days*, but I think I can relate to the views and hopes of the editor as he looks nostalgically to the past. Looking back after seventy-five years, the meaningful connections of my life certainly aren't difficult to identify. Though the memories of one's experiences may be commonplace, those memories, tempered by time, are significant in part because they are personal. And though those memories, like arrowheads, may be remnants of another time, they have a personal story to tell. I was reminded of this as I watched the extensive television coverage of the fiftieth anniversary observance of the allied invasion of Europe at Normandy during World War II. I was impressed by the personal stories many of the veterans had to tell and by the hell of those first few days of fighting on the beaches. I was struck also with the row upon row of white marble crosses in the military cemetery where almost 10,000 American dead from that invasion lay buried.

Though the military has been a significant and long-time connection for me, I discovered that I knew next to nothing about the specifics of the D-Day invasion. My memories, my arrowheads, of that time had to do with tramping around in the rain and mud in New Guinea and fighting both the Japanese and the scourges of a skin malady the medics called "jungle rot." In hyping the anniversary coverage, however, journalists almost forgot the larger war, especially that part of the fighting taking place on the other side of the world. But I shall never forget.

One of the broadcast commentators during the "D-Day Plus 50" coverage remarked that most of the veterans, now in their seventies, a few in their eighties, had sacrificed so much in their youth, even those who had survived the war. Most grew up during the years of the Great Depression, which had denied them the opportunities which most young people have today, and the war itself had denied many of them years of normal livelihood with family and in establishing civilian careers. And I recognized the commentator was talking about me, also.

The depression years were a part of that "hearty experience" which the *Good Old Days* editor made reference to, and the war indeed did deny me all those months with family and friends, four years and ten months to be exact. But from the military connection there has flowed opportunities for study and career advancement which would never have occurred otherwise.

When I graduated from high school in 1936, a farm boy of seventeen, there was little opportunity to attend college, which was not unusual. Indeed, before 1940 only about five percent of all Americans, really an elitist group, had ever been to college. Thanks to military service during World War II, I became eligible for school under the Servicemen's Readjustment Act of 1944, popularly called the G.I. Bill of Rights. It turned out that I was eligible for the maximum benefits, four years, which stretched to five nine-month academic years, sufficient for gaining both a bachelor's and master's degree in journalism at the University of Missouri.

This training in the halls of academe led to newspapering and, after twelve years of publishing, to further study for a doctorate and teaching at Southern Illinois University at Carbondale. During those later years of teaching journalism, there was a feeling of a career going full circle as veterans of the Vietnam War trickled into my classes under a more recent G.I. Bill. But while I went halfway around the world to gain eligibility for schooling under the original G.I. Bill, it turns out that my hometown, Salem, Illinois, through the effort of members of the American Legion Post and others, lays claim as the "birthplace" of the original document formulating the ideas for the legislation.

Helen and I recently attended an observance in Salem marking the fiftieth anniversary of the enactment of the federal statute. *The Salem Times-Commoner* published a special supplement for the occasion, for which I wrote an article, and money was being raised to erect a monument designating Salem as the "Birthplace of the G.I. Bill of Rights."

Writing about one's meaningful connections is one thing, but publication of such retrospection may result in an entirely unexpected experience. There we were recently on the front page of the

Times-Commoner peeking through a red heart with a byline story relating the romance of Harry and Helen in Salem that summer of 1940. I had been working on the essay on our marital connection for this manuscript when the newspaper invited readers to submit stories of their romances for a planned Valentine's Day edition. I lifted a few paragraphs for publication from this essay never expecting to win. Helen and I visited Salem recently to claim our prizes—dinner for two at Austin's, which we enjoyed with best friends Herman and Maxine Branson, then an overnight stay at our first ever bed and breakfast in the Badollet House's beautifully decorated suite where we feasted on a gourmet breakfast prepared by our host. Finally, there was a box of chocolates from Bandy's Pharmacy. It turned out to be a romantic visit, which we enjoyed immensely, but there was more.

Her name was Patricia Bauer, a young woman with a degree in communications from the University of Illinois and a major in advertising. As proprietor of the Badollet House, she operated a picture framing business on the first floor of the old red brick building, which had once served as a creamery, and her pictures and wall hangings overflowed into the B&B suite. She resided on the second floor with her husband, a banker with Boatmen's in Mount Vernon, and her four children, the oldest of them eleven. Pat was a gracious host, full of energy and enthusiasm, an excellent cook and, although not a native of Salem, a virtual repository of historical information about the area. Despite all her duties and responsibilities, Pat was involved in another major project, the renovation of the near-by two-story brick Italinate house, once an area showplace now fallen into disrepair.

I remember the place as the home of a boyhood acquaintance, Rich Howard, who was reared there by his uncle and aunt, John and Eva White. Rich and I served together in Company I during World War II. He survived the war only to be murdered a few years later in California in connection with his duties as a drug enforcement agent. But Pat knew the house from her research as the first brick home in Salem, built for Howard and Tabitha Badollet in 1854 on a one-acre wooded lot that included her creamery. It had served as a stop on the underground railroad for escaped slaves during the Civil War. John Scopes, defendant in the famous 1925 Scopes monkey trial in Tennessee, had boarded there while he was attending high school in Salem. Pat and her husband had purchased the dilapidated house in 1989 from the White estate and this summer of 1994 was to see it restored to its original beauty. What an arrowhead from the past Pat had discovered and was salvaging for future visitors of the Badollet Bed and Breakfast.

Speaking of the concept of time, our Sunday

School teacher, who generally poses more questions than he ever gets around to answering, frequently suggests that maybe the division of time into past, present, and future is only a contrivance of man and that all three, i.e., past, present, and future, may indeed be occurring at the same time. Helen may be getting at the same thing when she complains, as she sometimes does, that there isn't enough time to accomplish all that she wishes to do. My response generally is that we all have the same amount of time—twenty-four hours a day. But that may be more true for seventy-some seniors than for many others. I remember, for example, all the lives cut short by wars and violence and disease.

The most shocking story coming out of the news coverage of the Midwest floods of 1993 was the exhumation of hundreds of coffins—one report said more than six hundred—by floodwaters from a rural cemetery near Hardin, Missouri. The macabre action of the raging water brought bizarre news photos of dozens of the caskets floating down the Missouri River toward St. Louis with still others scattered haphazardly along Missouri Route 10. One reporter wrote that the scene evoked thoughts of doomsday, death, burial, and what, if anything, is ever permanent or concluded. The past, it seemed, had joined hands with the present, or maybe it was the initial stage of the Biblical resurrection of the dead, which in its early stages had somehow gone awry. Weeks later, the coffins were gathered up and, because of difficulty in identification, were reburied in a mass grave.

My favorite journalism professor at the University of Missouri, Frank Luther Mott, wrote a little book of biographical essays after he retired called *Time Enough*, a book similar to this one. He suggested that there was time enough to do what one wished to do if one would only make the time to do it. He told of setting his alarm to go off fifteen minutes early in order to have the time to read a chapter of a gift book aloud to his wife each morning at the breakfast table. But there isn't always "time enough," nor was there for Dean Mott.

I remember that as a graduate student in his "Literature of Journalism" seminar we often met in the Mott home where his extensive library was available to us. He had recently received a Pulitzer Prize for Volumes II and III of his projected six-volume *History of American Magazines* and was then working on Volume IV. But he had other projects underway as well, which he talked about to us, and he seemed to be delaying research on his magazine project, almost as if he hoped this would prolong his career and perhaps his life. He died in 1964 while still at work on Volume V, which was later published with the editorial assistance of his daughter. Those five volumes occupy a prominent place on a bookshelf in my study, but Volume VI, sadly, cut short by death, will never be published.

Books have fascinated me for as long as I can remember, but I suppose that my connection with publishing and teaching through the years have further encouraged this attraction to the printed word. I still enjoy poking around at book sales on campus when the University Book Store, the SIU Press, or the Friends of Morris Library hold sales to rid themselves of excess books, which they frequently do. When textbooks are put on sale, I'm reminded of how quickly such books can become obsolete. Scholarship, particularly in the professional disciplines, is like that; a few years out of the classroom and new knowledge displaces findings that were once at the cutting edge of research.

When the SIU Press holds a sale and one finds his own book, which was years in the research and writing, on sale for three dollars, one is reminded how ephemeral the glory of authorship can be. For librarians there is a concept of the shelf life of books, which seems an apt metaphor for living as well. When an individual is no longer useful or no longer has anything to contribute, it appears futile to argue that his shelf life should be extended.

So as a matter of defense, I have attempted to appear useful, and I've even contributed here and there. Helen and I for several years in retirement have delivered meals on wheels to shut-in Carbondale residents, most of them seniors, but arthritic knees have slowed this activity. We both work in two or three Red Cross blood drives each year, but the fear of AIDS and of the possibility of contaminated blood has removed my favorite job from the list of those performed by Red Cross volunteers— assembling the packets. And we support the programs of United Methodists, most of them anyway.

But since retirement, I suppose I spend more time keeping up academic contacts, writing letters of recommendations for former students and faculty colleagues, and pursuing various research projects. First there was the effort to revise *Editorial and Persuasive Writing* for a second edition published by Hastings House in 1990. And since retirement, I also have attempted to keep legal research skills honed, co-authoring various scholarly papers with former graduate students.

Two former doctoral students in particular, Don Sneed, now the chair of the Department of Journalism at Ole Miss, and Kyu Ho Youm, an associate professor of journalism at Arizona State, have been involved in most of these recent research efforts. Together we have produced legal papers presented at various scholarly conferences, primarily at the annual conference of the Association for Education in Journalism and Mass Communication, papers generally turned into articles for publication in a law journal or law review. Early on, Don and Kyu may have benefited from such efforts on my part, but now each has his own impressive publication record but continues the collaboration, a kindness to their former mentor. In the jargon of the librarian, I trust all this activity, scholarly and otherwise, will work to extend my shelf life.

It is leisurely reading, however, which takes less effort than writing, that I have found to be of continuing enjoyment through the years. Indeed, I now have a director's chair set up opposite my desk to take advantage of the light from a sliding door in my study. There is generally a book on the floor beside the chair. A leather slip cover, purchased years ago on sale at a religious book store, protects the book. Its soft leather feels good to my arthritic fingers as I hold the volume to read.

Recently I've been pursuing the memoirs of James Reston, a former *New York Times* editor and a two-time Pulitzer Prize winner for diplomatic reporting, appropriately entitled *Deadline*. Reston's Calvinist ancestors probably would be amused that I have his rather provocative memoirs wrapped in a Bible cover. Scotty, for many years the *Times* Washington bureau chief, had a fifty-year career in American journalism marked by deadlines. Deadlines can serve as a warning that things must be accomplished before a certain time, and most of us need that.

It's even said by hospice care givers that knowledge of a terminal illness can heighten a patient's desire to make every day count. Even healthy seniors often feel that time may be running out, that this is their last chapter, and they double their efforts to make every day count for more. I can identify with that.

Time ran out this week for a long-time friend and associate. Helen and I returned to Carbondale recently after attending graveside services for Darwin Hiestand at the Bethlehem Baptist Church cemetery south of Salem. For more than fifty years, we had enjoyed the friendship of Darwin and Mary, who always seemed to know how to enjoy life despite the difficulties and complexities that my favorite psychiatrist, Scott Peck, so often writes about. It was an interesting memorial service, but like so much this unconventional couple did through the years, it was different.

There had been no service in Tennessee, their summer home for the past several years, and where Darwin had died. At the simple graveside service at Bethlehem, more than fifty family members and friends crowded around the grave site on new mown grass to hear two eulogies, one of them a touching piece written by a teenage granddaughter from Cincinnati and read by a family friend. A minister might have been more eloquent, but there is something poignant in the halting words of a teenager feeling for the first time the loss of a loved one. Then the Legionnaires took over for a brief military ceremony: the presentation of the folded American flag to Mary, the widow; three volleys from the firing squad with rifles pointed into a cloudless June sky; and then the mournful sounding of "Taps." A grandson, too young perhaps to understand the solemnity of the occasion, gathered up the spent cartridge casings as souvenirs and showed them to his mother.

That was it. There was no minister; there was no casket; there was no open grave. The family had carried the box of ashes from Tennessee, which was buried there on an empty cemetery plot near the graves of Mary's parents after the mourners had withdrawn. It was a brief goodbye, but for me and Helen, it had been a touching tribute to a long-time friend.

The graveside service had rekindled memories for both Helen and me. Mary and I had been members of Bethlehem as teenagers, and we were both baptized in a farm pond across the road from the church. The pond had long since dried up and was now overgrown with brush. Helen and Mary, who were kissing cousins, had spent many visits together during the long years of World War II. Darwin's military outfit had helped to build the Alaska Highway across Canada during the war where he received disabling injuries bouncing about on the heavy dirt-moving equipment, which resulted in the replacement of both hips and limited activity for most of his life. But this didn't keep him from boating and fishing and traveling.

On our first trip to Florida during the 1950s, we visited them in West Palm Beach where they then lived and were introduced to the delicacies of seafood and the night life of Miami Beach. South Florida seemed far less crowded back then, a more exciting place to visit with little fear of being the victim of crime. They eventually moved to Central Florida to escape such fears where we visited them in their double wide on Lake Eustis near Leesburg. We loved to sit on the lanai and watch the activity on the lake. Frequently, Darwin would take us across the lake in his bass boat for lunch at the marina, sometimes detouring to look for alligators sunning themselves along the shore or to explore the shallow water and plant life of a cypress grove.

Later, we visited them on Dale Hollow Lake, a huge TVA impoundment that sits astride the Tennessee and Kentucky border north of Cookeville. I remember late night fishing in the deep waters of the lake to avoid the July heat and of watching the hummingbirds at the feeder outside the window of the Star Point diner where we frequently had lunch. And there were early morning walks through Elder Plantation where they lived, and leisurely visits on the deck of their home overlooking the lake and watching the activity around the marina. From such remembrances, to use a phrase from one of Robert Waller's little books, comes "pleasant sorrows."

As I write these lines, I'm viewing a pair of cardinals exploring the bird fountain in the backyard outside my study. The bright plumage of the male first caught my eye as he flitted around the gray lava stones near the fountain and then perched on the rim to take a couple of quick drinks from the water. The female, with little to identify her species except for her pink beak and a touch of color along the edge of her wings, is less active, but she stays close by her mate. After a few minutes, the male flies off through the shrubbery and disappears from sight. Shortly afterward, she follows. I linger to watch, but neither of them returns.

I write this incident down because if this were a literary manuscript such a chance sighting at such a propitious time probably would be said to have some significant symbolic meaning. Writing as a journalist, which I freely acknowledge, it's not likely that anyone will take these scribblings for literature. Of course, the abrupt departure of the cardinals from my bird fountain may merely suggest that the open road beckons and that it's time for Helen and me to pack up the New Yorker, which already has turned over 100,000 miles, and strike out on a journey down one of those "blue highways" William Least Heat Moon describes so magnificently in his 1982 bestseller detailing his "Journey into America," perhaps a road leading to a place where egrets fly.

My favorite niece, Beverly, for whom I write, may hold with neither of these interpretations, but clearly this personal narrative, like all tales, must end somewhere though the journey promises to continue—at least for a while longer.

Index